Lisa's gut-wrenching, transparent description of a tale walked out far too often, pulls you in, opens your eyes and gets your head nodding. Working 25 years in the Department of Corrections, ten as a warden, I saw firsthand the manifestation of unresolved trauma. I was inspired by her words and her journey. I believe this book will be an excellent tool for those wanting a way out of their hopelessness. I can't wait to put this book in the hands of numerous programs with men and women who I know will benefit from it and come away believing their lives can change. And for those of you who are unaware of these realities, this book will give you a firsthand intimate and uncensored glance. I guarantee it will help you to understand what really happens to the often forgotten person. Sadly, you already know them.

—John Charles Thomas
Global Director, Prison Ministry/Every Man a Warrior

In this book Lisa reveals her life story and struggles from childhood to adult life. You hear about the suffering that many experience living without love in a family. This compelling story is an excellent tool for victims, teachers and professionals dealing with this crisis. Lisa reveals everything, then shows how she began her climb out of misery to a life that can give satisfaction and love.

As a professional working with offenders for 50 years, it was a story that we need to hear that can help us with individuals we encounter.

—Terry L. Davis
Owner, Keystone Correctional Services;
retired Director of Adult Probation

Lisa Kessler-Peters invites you on a healing journey in her new book, *How I Learned to Hide*. Lisa's deep brokenness began as a child and continued into adulthood. Reading her healing process will start to break the stronghold of pain, giving you hope and practical steps to receive your healing.

—Cindy Stewart
Author and Senior Leader at The Gathering with Jesus

Lisa Kessler-Peters has written a must-read, detailed personal story that takes readers on a trauma-filled, dark and distorted journey that can be painful at times because of the raw truth it unravels. As a writer and a community psychologist, I can speak to the principles and experiences that she offers and to the healing that can be had through perseverance, education and resilience. We must not stop at the pain and seek to hide from our past, but we must engage in the faith of a better tomorrow by understanding how we got to the pain in the first place. Although we are taught that we are the problem and should be ashamed or afraid, the truth is we are God's children and therefore we are enough and we are good—i.e., we are good enough! We have gifts and talents that are ours since birth, and no amount of grief or shame can over-power us as long as we believe. Finally, God will take us from glory to glory as long as we continue to tell the story of love and redemption.

—Boris Hines, MA
Community Psychologist

Memoirs by those directly impacted by draconian and useless laws are among the most important ways for the public to understand their devas-tating and human impact. Lisa Kessler-Peters tells her story with honesty and genuine self-reflection, and it is important for those advocating for change to hear the voices of those most personally harmed by these inef-fective and cruel policies.

—Emily Horowitz, PhD
Professor & Chair, Department of Sociology and Criminal Justice
Co-Director, Justice Initiative
at Saint Francis College

HOW I LEARNED TO HIDE

Unraveling Shame and Rejection

LISA KESSLER-PETERS

Foreword by Chris and Carol Green

Paperback ISBN 978-1-960007-10-0
eBook ISBN 978-1-960007-11-7

Published by
Mercy & Moxie, an imprint of
Orison Publishers Inc.
PO Box 188, Grantham, PA 17027
www.OrisonPublishers.com

Scripture quotations marked (MSG) are taken from THE MESSAGE, copyright ©1993, 2002, 2018 by Eugene H. Peterson. Used by permission of NavPress. All rights reserved. Represented by Tyndale House Publishers, a Division of Tyndale House Ministries.

Scripture quotations marked (NIrV®) are taken from the Holy Bible, NEW INTERNATIONAL READER'S VERSION®. Copyright © 1996, 1998 Biblica. All rights reserved throughout the world. Used by permission of Biblica. NEW INTERNATIONAL READER'S VERSION® and NIrV® are registered trademarks of Biblica. Use of either trademark for the offering of goods or services requires the prior written consent of Biblica.

Scripture quotations marked (TPT) are taken from The Passion Translation®. Copyright © 2017, 2018, 2020 by Passion & Fire Ministries, Inc. Used by permission. All rights reserved. ThePassionTranslation.com.

Dedication

I dedicate this book to the child living inside each one of you who is still learning how to fully heal and live his or her best life. *You are enough!* You are so loved beyond what you can ever wrap your mind around. Your heavenly Father created you out of love. No matter what your earthly parents did or didn't do for you, remember that your life matters and that you are worth the work it takes to heal. I love you, and I am here for you!

Acknowledgments

I want to thank everyone who encourages and supports the calling that God has placed on my life. I also want to say thank you to those who have checked in on where I am in my writing process and encouraged me to keep going. To my children and my husband, thank you for being my biggest cheerleaders, as I am yours.

A special thank-you goes to Dr. Kathryn Whiteley, criminologist and producer of the documentary *Until We Have Faces*. Thank you for your encouragement and assistance with adding theory to my work. Most importantly, thank you for your friendship and for dedicating your life to telling the stories of those who have no voice to speak. You give them a voice.

Foreword

L isa is like an instrument in the hands of a skilled surgeon in the way she navigates the fine line between education, experience and faith. She brings forth knowledge and wisdom for those who are struggling every minute of every day in the aftermath of trauma, neglect, addictions and so many other overwhelming issues that are destroying people today.

Her sensitivity to explain clinical terms minimizes any feelings of intimidation for those who will read this book, and it brings understanding and hope for those who are living with shame and rejection. In the most remarkable way, she encourages and empowers those who are walking alongside family, friends or colleagues who are still in hiding.

We highly recommend this book for people-helpers in all professions, no matter how long they have been working in their field of expertise. It's time for all to come out of hiding, even those of us who are in the daily work to guide, coach, counsel or console others. This book must be in your library, and it must be referenced often.

Chris and Carol Green
Owners of C and C Connections, LLC
Certified Mental Health and Life Coaches

Contents

Introduction

Have you ever heard a voice inside your head tell you that you're worthless and unlovable? Have you ever had someone you love, such as a parent or spouse, tell you that everything you do is wrong and that you'll never get it right? There are so many defeating thoughts and words that tear you down. All of them make you feel useless, hopeless and beyond help. Those thoughts and words will tell you that you cannot come back from the mess you made or from what's been done to you. They say that you are too far gone, that you might as well continue numbing yourself with whatever habit you have taken up to cope, or, worse yet, that you should take your life.

All of these thoughts and words are lies. But they are some of what float around in your head and sometimes even come out of people's mouths at you. To answer the question you are thinking right now, *No, you are not alone in this!* I, too, dealt with these lies and did try to numb my hurt, even to the point of attempting suicide more than once.

Where do these lies come from? Why do we experience such awful torment? The answer is easy and hard. The easy answer is that satan is the source. (I don't capitalize his name intentionally, because he doesn't deserve it; he has no authority here.) He comes *only* to kill, steal and destroy, like the Bible says. Satan, himself, cannot just come right out and kill us; instead, he has us do the job for him. He uses what appear to be our own thoughts and the words and actions of others to get us to our low point. Satan does not walk up to us and identify himself. Rather, he is manipulative and cunning and typically uses people we love to try to destroy us.

I know this might be hard to follow if you are not sure if you believe in God and satan or any of that, but keep reading, and I will help unpack all of this for you.

Our low point is where we start to commit **self-destructive** acts or, even worse, try to take our own lives. Those self-destructive behaviors sometimes include quitting something important, such as work or school, or leaving our family. Sometimes those behaviors are beginning a habit that we said we would never take up, like smoking, doing drugs, drinking or engaging in self-harm. **Deliberate self-harm** includes a lot of different actions and behaviors, such as **cutting**, burning, overeating, starving (**anorexia**), binging and purging (**bulimia nervosa**), engaging in sexual promiscuity, and, worst case, actually attempting suicide. Sometimes the behavior manifests toward others, as in violent and homicidal behaviors. Self-destructive behaviors normally feel very good while we are engaged in them. They numb us and take us away from the pain we do not want to feel. However, when we are done making a mess, we are stuck with the consequences of that behavior. Still, most of us repeat the behavior over and over, running around in a circle of self-destructiveness just trying to avoid ourselves.

I know the pain that comes with believing these lies, and I know it is hard to recognize when a thought is a lie. That thought feels real. Those words sound real. That thought and those words hurt and are heavy. It feels like the air is pushed right out of your lungs, and it is hard to breathe. It is hard to get out of bed when those thoughts swim around inside your mind. People have so many thoughts in a day, literally thousands of them, and many of them are negative. Those whispers of low self-worth and rejection play on repeat if you don't know how to stop them. They can make you feel crazy, and sometimes you indeed have a mental breakdown. I know. I've been there.

To add to the pain, you stay silent. At this point you do not want anyone to know that you think those crazy thoughts. You feel as if you are the problem, that this is an isolated situation that involves only you, and no one else can be feeling this way. You think that if you tell people, they will reject you even more. Maybe they will make fun of you or push you further away for feeling this way. Or maybe, you think, they will lock you up and throw away the key! Again let me tell you, *these are lies* that the enemy (another term used for satan or the devil) uses to keep you in torment. It is a living hell to be trapped inside of yourself, feeling alone in your pain. I've experienced it. People don't seem safe to talk to because you fear what they will think, say or do in response when you tell them what's going on, and that makes you feel even more rejected.

Education has been a big part of my healing process. It has helped me to understand what is going on inside my own brain and body. It also has equipped me to help others in a more impactful way. I am dedicated to not purposefully causing more harm to others, if possible. Thus I have added some additional educational theory to this book in simplified terms to help you learn what helped me. Sections titled "Going Deeper" contain more in-depth information. The terms that are presented in bold type are defined in a glossary at the end of the book, if you want to learn more. My goal is to help you so you, too, can heal; or, if you love or work with individuals enduring these issues, to equip you so you can know better what is going on in that person's thinking.

In my first book, *Why I Tried to Die: A Story of Trauma, Resilience and Restoration*, I described what happened to me and what I did and thought and felt all the way through to my healing. In this book, I also use my lived experience combined with my education to share what happens and how you can get your breakthrough and stop repeating behavior patterns that keep you stuck. The process of healing is not easy or short. Believe me, I wish it were. I know it seems easier just to numb the pain, to push it away or down, to put it in a box and say that you will just leave it there. Unfortunately, not dealing with it does not make it go away. It is still there. It still affects your life in very real ways, whether or not you are aware of it. Sometimes people develop anger issues, isolate, have control issues, avoid or become over-sensitive. People can develop all types of reactions to pain to try to make it go away. The reality is, no matter what you do and where you go, you take yourself with you. If you don't deal with it, you will find yourself running from yourself your entire life.

Are you ready? If so, put your seatbelt on and let us travel into transparency with one another and do some healing.

Going Deeper

A painful "thought life" can stem from childhood **trauma**. One of the most important factors that can determine how children grow up thinking about themselves is the environment they are raised in. Trauma was not always a well-studied part of mental health. Originally research was focused on those who had been to war. It wasn't until the 1990s when the first study was conducted of how abuse and dysfunction within a family unit affected individuals. The study examined the first 18 years of a child's life and how those factors could impact that child in adulthood. This study referred to these factors as Adverse Childhood Experiences or ACEs. The study is simply a short questionnaire that you can find online today. It has become a part of assessing trauma in a child's or an adult's life. The questions ask about such things as witnessing and experiencing abuse and having parents who experienced mental health issues, had a **substance use disorder**, or were incarcerated at some point in the child's life.

Researchers studied the correlation between ACE scores and many physical, mental, social and cognitive issues. It showed that the higher the ACE score was, the more likely an individual was to have chronic health problems, mental illness and substance use issues. It showed that ACEs negatively impact an individual's ability to work and to have healthy relationships and increase the individual's likelihood of engaging in risky behaviors. Worst of all, high ACE score indicates that the longevity of life is shortened. Following is a chart that depicts these conclusions.

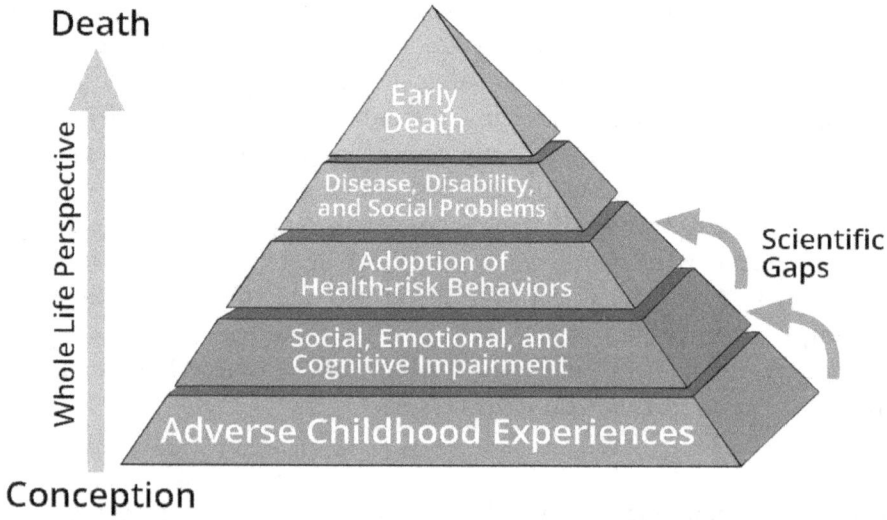

Figure 1: This pyramid shows how adverse childhood experiences can potentially affect individuals throughout their lifespans (The ACE Pyramid, 2014)

I want to be clear: I scored a ten on my ACEs questionnaire. That is the highest score you can have. I have used this questionnaire as a tool to better understand myself and what I am up against so that I can heal and do better for myself and my children. I have not allowed it to make me feel defeated by my childhood. This questionnaire is to help us know better so we can do better. I do a lot of things now in my life to try and reverse the toll of these traumas on my body, mind and soul. Feeding my body properly, exercising, tending to my mental health, and learning more about what has happened to me are some of the things I do to reverse the effects of my adverse childhood experiences. I invite you to do the same. We are resilient people! We can and will overcome our adverse childhood experiences!

1
You Don't SEE Me!

When my son was a toddler, around the age of two, he started doing the cutest thing. Whenever it was time to get undressed to get in the bath or to get changed, he would cover his own eyes tight with both his chunky little hands and mutter, "You don't see me!" It would make me giggle and laugh, and I would say, "You're right! Now it's time to get dressed." Then I would help his little arms and legs into his clothes. Like most toddlers, his head seemed so much bigger than his body, and it would barely fit through the hole in his shirt. As a team, we would squeeze his head through. His sandy-blond hair would pop through, then his big blue eyes would meet my brown eyes, and we would smile. This memory still makes me smile and giggle because it was so innocent and sweet. Obviously, my son was trying to say, "Do not look at me," and desiring privacy. I never thought anything of it at the time, other than that my toddler was absolutely adorable.

As I started looking at the topic of **shame** and **rejection**, God reminded me of this sweet memory and made me realize that it was embarrassment that caused my son to cover his eyes. He was thinking that I could not see him if he covered his eyes. It seems to make no sense at first glance why a young child would be embarrassed about being naked. Now, I know this is not the case for all children. Some toddlers very much love to run around with nothing on, but I want to make a different point here.

Children grow so much in the first five years of life. They start to develop individual personality traits and characteristics beyond the early stages of infancy, when their only concern is for the immediate needs of love, food, sleep, comfort, gas relief and a dry diaper. There is a good bit of research that supports the thought that around the age of 18 to 24 months (about two years), children start to become self-aware. "For instance, they now begin to use pronouns—I, me, mine—to refer to themselves. They may begin to use proper names, including their own. They are also increasingly capable of empathic acts, demonstrating their increased sense of being an object who can be experienced by another" (Holinger 2012). I think one of the major transitions that happens here is that children start to recognize themselves as people who are separate from their caregivers. (I will talk later about attachment to caregivers in early childhood and how that affects someone's ability to have healthy relationships.)

What I want you to remember is this; we only start to develop embarrassment and shame and fear rejection when we become aware of ourselves as individuals.

2
In the Beginning

In my study of shame and rejection, God brought me to the very begin-ning of the Bible to a story most of the world is aware of, whether or not they believe it to be true. It is the story of the creation of the world and of man and how God said the world was good and the creation of man was very good. If you look at Genesis chapter 3, just three chapters into the Bible, though, the story takes a turn for the worse. Satan, in the form of a serpent, tricks the first man and woman, Adam and Eve, into disobeying God.

Have you ever daydreamed of going back and telling Eve the truth about what was going on and that she shouldn't listen to the serpent? I have! I also have thought, *Great. If this Bible is real, then this stupid woman ate from the tree and messed up, and now we all must pay the cost forever.* It left me feeling powerless to think that someone else's mistake is why my life is such a wreck and that I cannot do anything about it. I have even felt angry about it. *That isn't fair! Why is it like that?* However, it is of the utmost importance that you do not take part of the Bible and make it the whole truth. Keep in mind that it is just a part of the whole.

In Genesis chapter 3, Eve gave the fruit to her husband, and they ate it. The serpent was able to put doubt in Eve's mind, making her believe that her Creator was keeping something good from her, when in fact God was protecting her purity and goodness. The very first thing that happened after Adam and Eve ate the fruit was that they became aware of their nakedness and were embarrassed. Before that, in the very last sentence of chapter 2 of Genesis, the Bible states, "The two of them, the Man and his Wife, were na-ked, but they felt no shame" (MSG).

After satan brought doubt of God's goodness, shame was the very next tactic satan used to bring ruin to man. What followed was rejection. Satan pits us against ourselves from the very beginning, whispering tormenting lies like, "You are naked and exposed. God can see what you have done, and He is angry! Hide yourself from Him. He will no longer love you for what you have done. You are bad! You are unloved!" How many of us have heard this petrifying death sentence whispered in our ear? Worse yet, how many of us have believed it? I have!

Here's the story in Genesis 3:1–13:

> The serpent was clever, more clever than any wild animal God had made. He spoke to the Woman: "Do I understand that God told you not to eat from any tree in the garden?"
>
> The Woman said to the serpent, "Not at all. We can eat from the trees in the garden. It's only about the tree in the middle of the garden that God said, 'Don't eat from it; don't even touch it or you'll die.'"
>
> The serpent told the Woman, "You won't die. God knows that the moment you eat from that tree; you'll see what's really going on. You'll be just like God, knowing everything, ranging all the way from good to evil."
>
> When the Woman saw that the tree looked like good eating and realized what she would get out of it—she'd know everything!—she took and ate the fruit and then gave some to her husband, and he ate.
>
> Immediately the two of them did "see what's really going on"—saw themselves naked! They sewed fig leaves together as makeshift clothes for themselves.
>
> When they heard the sound of God strolling in the garden in the evening breeze, the Man and his Wife hid in the trees of the garden, hid from God.
>
> God called to the Man: "Where are you?"
>
> He said, "I heard you in the garden and I was afraid because I was naked. And I hid."

God said, "Who told you that you were naked? Did you eat from that tree I told you not to eat from?"

The Man said, "The Woman you gave me as a companion, she gave me fruit from the tree, and, yes, I ate it."

God said to the Woman, "What is this that you've done?"

"The serpent seduced me," she said, "and I ate" (MSG).

When we look at this story, we see that there was no shame until they ate from the tree of the knowledge of good and evil. Why would that have caused them shame? Maybe it was because they were disobedient to their Creator and felt separated from Him. Maybe it was because they felt embarrassed and guilty, which caused them to feel badly. Whatever the reason, this feeling made them hide, just like a young child does when that child does something wrong. When we feel shame, we are afraid of being rejected and often project that to be the outcome before it even happens. We paint a picture of the outcome—a picture that says we are no longer lovable. I propose that these are the feelings Adam and Eve had in the garden after eating from the forbidden tree. I believe they were full of shame, expected rejection and felt unloved. They opened themselves up to the lies of the enemy, satan. I will also go so far as to say that I believe God was not angry but brokenhearted. Their consequences were not the result of His anger but were a result of being opened to good and evil.

Adam and Eve were naked since the day they were created. God created us to be naked—to be exposed and vulnerable. Our nakedness represents our transparency and vulnerability. God is not far away from us, angry with us. God is here with us, full of compassion. God and His Spirit have been here among us since the creation of the world. God became man to show us the way back to Him. Jesus is the image of God in man. Jesus is fully God and fully man. Once we learn the character of Jesus, we can understand the heart of God. When we are walking with God, obedient to His direction because He knows what is best for us, we will not have shame and rejection. We will have quite the opposite: humility and acceptance. Shame and rejection are the result of not knowing who we are in Christ Jesus. Shame is the result of not believing in forgiveness for ourselves and for others. Rejection is the result of looking to people for acceptance. Unraveling shame and rejection in our lives takes some time, like peeling back the layers of an onion.

In this book I will share with you how shame and rejection are the two biggest tools satan uses to try to destroy us. He has been very successful at it as well; just *look at us*. We have been engulfed in his lies since the beginning of time. My hope is that through sharing my breakthrough and what I learned through education, I can help you find freedom from shame and rejection as well.

3
Fool Me Once, Shame on You

I remember—before my mom began leaving us kids alone to go to bars—how dearly I loved her. I remember her complaining about not liking how she looked because of giving birth to four kids, and I encouraged her to take care of herself. I remember being on the floor in the living room watching workout videos with her and copying what the instructor did on the video. I wanted my mom to feel good about herself. I loved her. I cared for her. She was my mommy, even with all her faults.

After she started leaving us alone to go out on the town at night, my thoughts toward her changed. I started thinking bad things, angry things, hurtful things about her. I didn't know it at the time, but it was because I was brokenhearted. She had abandoned and rejected me. It was the first time I had ever been rejected, and it was very painful.

To this day, 30-plus years later, I can still feel my heart physically hurting in my chest at her rejection, just as it did in the beginning. I remember thinking, *Why won't she love us? Why aren't we good enough for her?* I remember not being able to bear that rejection and turning it into hate. Can you relate?

The truth is, we all have been rejected at some point in our lives. Some people have been rejected a lot more than others. I believe that the earlier in childhood this rejection happens and the greater the degree of closeness of the person doing it (i.e., a parent) play a huge part in the level of damage it can cause. Yes, it hurts when a boy on the playground rejects you, but it's a whole other thing when the woman who carried you in her womb behaves in a way that says, "I don't want you anymore." My safety net had a hole in it, and I didn't know what to do to fix it to feel safe again.

Sometimes this abandonment is an actual separation, a physical abandonment that occurs. Other times it is an emotional abandonment. Children like me who have grown up in many different homes with many different people develop numerous survival skills. The mental health field refers to these survival skills as **defense mechanisms.** The one that kept me alive was telling myself that I was indeed all alone and that no one was going to help me. It made me feel alone, yet it also made me pull my strength from within, knowing I had no one I could depend on but myself. I was going to have to do everything on my own. I trusted no one. I told people what they wanted to hear. I so deeply wanted someone to love and care about me, yet I believed the lie that I was unloved and unwanted. I was so lonely all the time.

In full transparency, I will tell you that to this day I still struggle with the remnants of this defense mechanism. When people are trying to be kind to me in a time of difficulty, it comes across to me as pity, and I tell myself, *I do not need it.* This thinking causes little Lisa to want to get defensive and combative. Living in this survival mode for all my life has made it difficult for me to develop trusting relationships. If I am always looking to get rejected, then that is what I am going to receive, because it is the perspective I have painted for myself to see.

There are so many scenarios that can cause this feeling of abandonment. Having a mother or father who is absent physically is a common one. Being raised in foster care is a huge one, especially when children have multiple homes that they bounce around in. Never being adopted is another. Sometimes even landing in a group home or detention center because of a lack of places for foster children to go to causes the feeling of being abandoned. Also, having a parent struggle with a substance-use disorder, a mental health diagnosis or a toxic relationship, or just being a workaholic—basically, anything that causes a parent to not be present either emotionally or physically—can cause a child to feel abandoned. I think sometimes we underestimate the fact that a family can look like it is well put together, yet still be a toxic environment.

Sometimes the demands that parents place on children can be too much, such as placing our own expectations of success on our children. A lot of times we try to overcompensate for whatever was missing or lacking in our own upbringing. If we grew up poor, for instance, then we might think financially providing for our kids is the most important thing we do. But if it causes us to work 80 hours a week and we are only home to sleep, we are still not present and are causing issues of neglect and abandonment.

As a mother, I can attest that it can be very difficult to balance providing for my family and being present. On more than one occasion, God has reminded me that my family is my first ministry, that I cannot be off trying to help the world and neglect my own family. My greatest calling is breaking patterns of trauma, addiction and abuse for my own family line.

Going Deeper

I think this is the perfect place to talk about **attachment theory** styles and how they affect an individual's ability to develop healthy relationships with others. Have you ever felt relationally challenged? Before I fully understood how my childhood trauma affected me, I felt like there was something fundamentally wrong with me. It seemed like I was cursed or broken or just unlucky. Although those are the words people use when they have these issues in relationships, such words still make people feel helpless in the situation. Sometimes people swing the pendulum to the other extreme and refuse to form any type of relationship at all. That is what I did! What educating myself in this area has taught me is that it is normal to have issues developing healthy relationships when you experienced abandonment in your childhood. Furthermore, it makes sense that you don't have the first clue what a healthy relationship looks like if no one ever modeled it for you. It makes sense that you are afraid people are not safe and believe that no one will ever stay around if that is what your history has shown you. Unfortunately, what people do as a reaction is push others away and then, when they aren't there, say, "See, I told you they wouldn't stay!" It's a **self-fulfilling prophecy**. This simply means you act in a way that gets the results you already believe are going to happen.

Attachment theory and the different attachment styles help to identify how children in early childhood bond with their caregivers. When children have attentive, loving parents who connect with them and provide for their needs, a secure attachment is able to be formed. Unfortunately, when children are in an environment where their needs are not taken care of or where there is chronic stress or a caregiver isn't present, an insecure attachment is formed. Individuals who have secure attachments in childhood are more likely to have secure attachments in relationships as they grow up. As you can imagine, having insecure attachments in childhood can cause developmental delays and lead to many social and psychological barriers.

Learning this information put words to what was going on inside of me. This made me dig deeper into insecure attachments. I wanted to understand my attachment style, so I could help myself heal in this area of my life. There are three types of insecure attachments: preoccupied-anxious, dismissing-avoidant and fearful-disorganized. Figure 2 shows these attachment types in a model that I think makes them easier to comprehend.

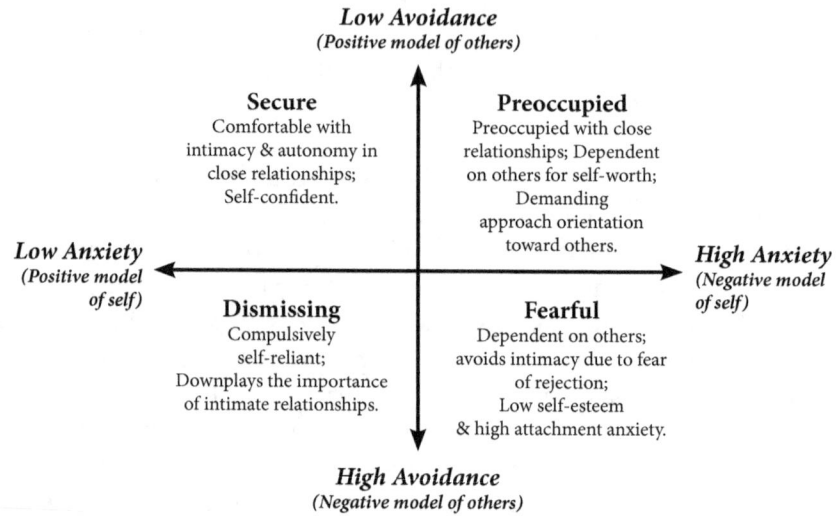

Figure 2: Model of attachment

My attachment style seems to fluctuate between dismissing and fearful, due to my childhood and the lack of proper, supportive parenting when I was young. The people who were supposed to be my safety were the people I feared. Today what that looks like for me is that I think people in general are unsafe. I prefer to be a lone wolf and take care of things on my own. I can even be guarded in my marriage. The hardest part of dealing with this thinking is that I desire to be in relationships with others, but I just find the risk to not be worth it. Other times I believe that people only want me around for what they can use me for. If you are interested in finding out what attachment type you deal with, there are online quizzes you can take.

Jesus truly has been the only one to break through this barrier completely; He is the only one I have let fully in. I now know my identity in Christ; therefore, I don't struggle with the low self-esteem and the feeling of not being good enough anymore. I do well in working with strangers and helping others when I know the relationship is one-sided. I am the helper, and they are the receivers of the help. Over time I have been able to develop a few close friends whom I know I can trust. This progress comes from being honest with myself and getting out of my comfort zone.

A few ways you can work on overcoming these attachment styles include sharing what is going on inside of you, trusting safe people in small increments, and refusing to push people away even when everything inside you is telling you to do so. In my opinion, trusting safe people is important. You must learn what safe people are and how to be a safe person yourself. One way to determine if a person is safe is to ask yourself, does this person allow me to be myself and accept me as I am without trying to change me into someone else? People can encourage you to be your best version of yourself, yet that should never include becoming who they want you to be. Safe people will not ask you to change to benefit them; instead, they will encourage you to change to benefit you. Finding safe people and being a safe person is a crucial part of starting to have healthy relationships.

4
Fool Me Twice, Shame on Me

When the rejection you experience comes from one individual, forgiveness can be difficult but obtainable, even if the damage was done over an extended period of time. However, when multiple people are part of the damage done, forgiveness becomes more complicated.

When my siblings and I went to live with my dad, I thought things would get better. I thought I could just put aside the fact that I had a mom who didn't want us and start my new life with my other parent. I literally heard these words come out of my mom's mouth about us to a police officer: "Take them; they are no good anyway, and I don't want them." Just imagine the pain that pierces through a child overhearing such a conversation. Or maybe you don't have to imagine it because you heard something similar.

Very quickly after our move, I realized that although life was much different, it was not in a good way. The whole premise for not living with my mom was that she would leave us home alone to go out. Now I lived in a home with two adults, my dad and my aunt (his sister), and *both* were absent, physically and emotionally. I started being a witness to crimes and sexual acts and was present at bars and wild parties. I never understood how those adults could not see us children there. In the bars, we would have to sit at a table while my dad sat at the bar drinking with his friends. Their crude conversations were filled with derogatory and obscene words. My introduction to what men thought of women and how they spoke about them still makes me nauseous.

It was as if the adults didn't notice we kids were even in the room. But *children observe everything going on around them*. Please don't be naïve enough to think that when they are in the presence of destruction, they witness nothing. They hear and see way more than you think. To the adult child reading this section and who was just triggered by this statement, I understand, and I am sorry. Just hold on; we will get through this together.

After being invisible in a room full of people for a while, you learn to hide. This hiding isn't a physical hiding; it is more of an emotional "breaking off." Children will start to separate how they actually feel from how they need to behave in order to survive. These survival skills keep people alive during crisis, abuse, neglect and so forth. The act of consciously trying to separate the painful feelings and thoughts is referred to as **suppression.**

Everyone always said I was a sweet, quiet girl. I was the child you would want to take with you because I wouldn't ask for anything, I didn't speak much, and I was helpful. No one knew what was going on inside me. As all these painful things were happening to me, no one ever talked about all the stuff going on. Eventually I believed that our life was just the way it was. I started believing that life was a horrible thing to endure. As much as I tried to keep myself hidden, the pain was overwhelming to my spirit, and my soul was being damaged.

The longer I stayed hidden, the more I separated from myself, and the lonelier I became. I did not realize that the pattern of rejection was repeating itself. At that age, all I knew was that I was the common denominator, that everything had to be my fault. Eventually I needed something to numb me and take me away from how I felt, since just suppressing it was not enough.

I remember how I would swing on swings, close my eyes and imagine myself flying away. I often ran away, only to remember I had nowhere to go and no one who cared or would even notice that I was gone. When I was in foster homes, I would think, *These people don't understand. They do not live in the real world and see things for how they really are. They live in these imaginary fantasies that are not real for people like me.* It made me so angry and sad.

Why did I get this life? I would often think about how unfair it all was. I was a good girl, yet all this horrible stuff happened to me. I started attempting suicide at the very early age of nine years old. None of the responses to my suicide attempts gave me a safe place to talk about what was going on inside of me. Instead, they caused that rejection monster to get bigger.

5
The Whisper

The enemy, satan, would whisper torment in my ear. "See, no one cares. There is no point in living. Just kill yourself!" There are more than seven billion people in the world, and satan is using the same tactic on most of us. Whether we endured great neglect as children or had a good upbringing with healthy parents, if satan was able to trip us up using the tactic of rejection, the pain was all very much the same. We cannot compare one life to another and say, "Well, you didn't endure childhood trauma, so your struggle with rejection is irrelevant." All pain is relevant.

I had my own struggle with this issue. For instance, my time in jail was very short compared with that of some of the people with whom I do advocacy work. Now, for those who don't know, there is a difference between county (jail) and state (prison) correctional institutions in the United States. The key difference is that jails are intended for short sentences and temporary confinement, while prisons are for sentences longer than a year. County jails are also where people are held while they await trial if they cannot pay their set bail to get out. Many people in county jails are not yet convicted of a crime and are considered innocent by law yet are treated like they are convicted criminals.

The impact of prison on me has been significant. Time moves very slowly on the inside, and my time felt long. At first I would dread when people asked me how long I was in prison, especially when I was in a room doing work with people who did 20-plus years. I struggled with whether my story had validity compared with the stories of others who spent long amounts of time incarcerated. It was a dear co-worker who spent four decades in prison who told me, "Your time is relevant to you and your story." I also do some solitary confinement work with people who have been on death row for decades

15

or who have endured long sentences in solitary confinement. Again, I felt unqualified in my experience compared with the torment they must have endured. After speaking with them, I realized that the pain is the same and relevant to each of us. Any time a person is put into a six-foot by eight-foot cage inside of a cement box and treated like an animal, it is inhumane and disregards the basic human need for human decency.

I remember when it became known at the prison that I was suicidal. It was not a desperate attempt to get out of prison; I was sincerely suicidal. I was not given any care or consideration. No help was offered or given. There was no safety plan put in place. Well, maybe they considered what they did to be a safety plan. I was put in an isolated cell by myself, with nothing but a wool blanket. They took my shoes, socks, glasses, bra, hair tie and even the toilet paper from my cell. I had a tan uniform and a light-gray, wool blanket. Everything else in the cell—bunk bed, toilet and sink—was bolted down. The cell was the size of my walk-in closet: six feet by eight feet. The floor was so filthy that I would use the corner of the blanket to scoot over to the toilet so that I did not have to put my bare feet on the floor. This was the same blanket I used to sleep with. I was not given a toothbrush, toothpaste, deodorant, a clean uniform or even a shower for a full week. I had a bright light on 24 hours a day. I would have to roll myself like a burrito in the blanket, trying to tuck in both my feet and my head to even attempt to sleep. I was not given any of my psychiatric meds, and when I asked for them, I was told, "You won't be getting any of that in here, honey." Then they laughed and walked away. When I would cry, I was told to shut the **** up. I had a blurry, thick-paned glass window in my cage, but I could see outlines of things through it. I remember crying as I saw a groundhog or a bird because it had more freedom than I did. And the enemy continued to whisper torment in my ear: "Just kill yourself. No one cares, even when they know you want to die. You are all alone. No one is coming to help you. You will only be free if you die. Others will never understand."

Regardless of what a person has done, this is inhumane treatment. Yet it is how inmates across our country are treated every day! If we took the time to hear the stories of those inside our prisons, our thoughts toward them would be very different. The pain and struggle that individuals go through prior to getting to the point of doing harm to others or breaking the law is what needs to be examined. People are not born evil. I know that a good number of people believe there are just some "bad apples," yet I know the Creator of us all, and *He* does not create bad things.

As a response to the hard experiences people go through in life, yes, some choose to live a life that is filled with evil and horrific actions. Some people do things that are unspeakable and inhumane. Do you ever ask yourself how they become that way? I guarantee you that they were not born that way. Instead, ask yourself, "What was their childhood like? Who were their parents? Were they supported? Were there mental health barriers that were not addressed as issues arose?"

We do not know what goes on inside people's brains if they do not reveal it. I know firsthand that it is hard to explain what is going on inside. What is shown on the outside is not always a good indicator of what is going on inside. Anger is usually the result of a completely different feeling. Some of those feelings include hurt, humiliation, rejection, fear and shame.

With that in mind, think of people who commit violent crimes out of anger. Not knowing what to do with their pain, it's just left there to fester. Then it comes out in ways that destroy other people's lives. Now, I am not justifying abuse or violence. I am simply trying to tell part of the story of what is happening a lot of the time. There are these vicious cycles of people hurting people, and those damaged people then hurt more people. It can go on and on from generation to generation if we do not stop it. And it is not as easy as saying, "I'm not going to be like my dad/mom," and stopping. As we all know from our own lives, it is not as easy as saying we won't do something. If we do not learn a different way of living, we will repeat the cycle! And in order to learn a new way of living, we must *unlearn* what we learned previously.

6
The Many Masks
We Wear

Prior to the world pandemic known as the coronavirus or Covid-19, we did not walk around wearing masks on our faces. Some people adapted to that protocol more easily than others. For me, it was difficult for three reasons. First, the mask made it hard for me to breathe. Second, I was silenced all my life, and I felt like the mask was a muzzle, trying to make me quiet. And third, I have worked so hard to remove the masks I have been wearing my entire life that it felt like I was losing all that ground I had gained. I found a good bit of information in the United Kingdom that supports and affirms my struggles of being a survivor of sexual abuse and wearing a mask. The Survivors Trust, an organization in the United Kingdom, even provided printable resources for a mask-exemption card due to one's survivor status ("Covid-19: Are You Concerned about Wearing a Mask?" n.d.). Unfortunately, I have not found any similar research or resources in the United States.

Rejection has a mask. Shame has a mask. My rejection mask often looked like I was fitting in and being liked by everyone in the room. It looked like "people pleasing" and being a chameleon. I would be whatever people wanted me to be. I was the life of the party. I played hard to get, and at the same time, knew that I was going to give myself away. I had no value for myself as a person. I was a classic case, as described in the following:

> "Hypersexualized behavior [is] a common reaction to pre-mature sexual exposure or a traumatic sexual experience. If a child is too young to be excessively masturbating or is engaging in pre-mature sexual play or behavior, this is typically a sign that the child has witnessed, been a participant in or has been exposed to

adult sexuality. In adolescence and adulthood, this can take the form of promiscuity, illegal sexual activity such as prostitution or participation in pornography, escort services, etc." (Bernard 2018).

One of the most tragic things about being a person who has been sexually abused is the shame you carry. This shame is twofold. First, it makes you feel unclean and want to hide. You feel filthy, and no matter how many times you wash, the filth won't come off. You feel ruined. You feel unlovable and untouchable. You replay every action and somehow conclude that you asked for it and did not even realize that you did. It could be something you did or did not say. It could be what you wore or a behavior you participated in. Your thoughts about healthy intimacy are ruined and distorted. **Sexual perversion** becomes normal to you (perversion meaning *distorted*.) *Distortion* is another word for twisted, false, misleading.

My first awareness of anything sexual was distorted. Before I was even ten years old, I witnessed an orgy, pornography with aggressive themes, and someone being sexually violated while she was passed out under the influence of alcohol. None of this perversion was ever talked about. At the same time, my dad would threaten me with chastity belts and make me swear in writing that I would wait until marriage to have sex. It was his way of trying to protect me from this world. (If only he knew what the future held.) By that point, though, my innocence was already gone. I had not been physically violated yet, but my soul was already damaged. I was around grown men talking inappropriately about women, and it did so much damage to hear adults talk in a way that was not honoring or protective. Their words were vulgar and crude. Even though I was not the one saying those things, I remember those words making me feel badly about who I was. Furthermore, I watched women live a risky, promiscuous lifestyle and not respect themselves. A child witnesses nothing good while hanging out in bars and at parties–watching people get drunk and making poor decisions.

As my siblings and I grew up in this environment, we took advantage of the opportunity provided by no parental guidance. We thought it was freeing to hang out with the grownups and see what they did. We laughed at their stupidity and drunkenness. All the while, as our little mouths laughed, our little souls were being crushed by the lack of proper parenting.

I remember wanting so much for my dad to get his life together, for him to give us the attention we needed. I can count on one hand the number of times my dad was present, cognitively present. When people are suffering from **addiction** (I use the words *addiction* and *substance use disorder* interchangeably), they are not present even when their body is physically there. They are impaired. I know this even from my own battle with addiction. Lander, Howsare and Byrne speak about the impact on the family when someone within the household suffers from substance use disorder. During the stages of life when attachment, security and safety should be reinforced, instead instability and fear are instilled in children with parents who have substance use disorder (Lander, et. al. 2013, 194-205).

If you are in an addiction, no matter how hard you want to be there, to be present, you just cannot. Instead you are hyperfocused on all the things related to your drug of choice. Life is out of control, and you want more than anything to be present, but you can't. Then when you fail, you feel shame. You feel badly, so you use more drugs/alcohol to numb the pain of failing. Those who want you to be present feel rejected. It is a lose/lose situation. No one wins, and the cycle plays on repeat.

The second part of the shame mask is not wanting to be seen. I just wanted to fade away. I often would physically hide, not wanting anyone to see how dirty and bad I actually was. Shame will have you believing that people can see what is going on inside of you. It makes you paranoid. Shame is brutal. It makes you want to just go away forever. It literally has people killing themselves every day just to get rid of it. Those left behind are rejected and abandoned. Those left behind feel like they were not enough for their loved one to stay around. Do you see how rejection and shame play this vicious, dirty, little game?

Once you have been struck with shame, you find yourself trying to overcompensate to please others. I often would think, *If I could just get someone to love me, I would be okay.* Being familiar only with the environment I was raised in and then being sexually abused by my father, I thought I had to have sex with someone in order for him to love me. I thought that my sexual intimacy would buy me love. It took a very long time for me to figure out that you cannot buy love, and that sex and love are not the same thing! Meanwhile, I devalued myself more and more. Every time I would give myself away and not be swept off my feet by Prince Charming, I was further rejected.

Every hit of rejection felt completely different, yet completely the same. Often it would result in an episode of depression and sometimes a suicide attempt. I never realized that it was layering itself, one rejection on top of another. Every time I felt rejection, it was not just that rejection—it also was the rejection from my mom, the rejection of my dad, then the rejection of his family, the rejection of this boy and that boy, and the rejection of those friends. And that just covers the first two decades of my life!

I kept waiting for someone to complete me. People often refer to their spouse or significant other as their "other half" or "better half." I have come to learn that I must be whole and healed myself before I can enter a relationship with someone else. I must have worth and value for myself before I can expect someone else to value me or see my worth. That does not mean I had to have it completely figured out; if that were the case, then I would still not be married. Marriage is built on each partner supporting the other and encouraging one another through the growth each is still undergoing. It does not mean fixing the other person. I wanted so badly for someone else to do the work for me, although I did not realize that while I was going through those times. If you had confronted me about it, I would have been super defensive. I felt it wasn't my fault that I was damaged; it was the fault of all the people who hurt me, so someone else had to fix me. This is the furthest thing from the truth.

You see, I was a caretaker of others. I had **codependency**. Codependency appears in a relationship in which there is a "giver" and a "taker." In codependency, one's value comes from taking care of other people and pleasing them, and I've had that need my entire life. There was no time for me to take care of myself, and that was way too exhausting. I felt like no one cared about me. No one in my family talked about their feelings when I was growing up. Advocating for myself was an impossible thing for me to do up until my mid-30s. For sure it is something I am continuously working on. I still have to remind myself that I am worth it and that I never deserve to be mistreated, regardless of my past mistakes.

One thing to learn is that there are roles within dysfunctional families. One of the family roles that emerges is the caretaker. In this role, a child becomes partially responsible for a parent who has substance use disorder, because it becomes clear to that child that the parent cannot care for himself or herself.

Going Deeper

There are many roles within a **dysfunctional family**. A dysfunctional family is typically one that has to adapt their roles because of the parents' inability to parent properly for whatever reason. Examples of parenting inability are when a parent is in substance use disorder, has a mental illness or suffers a major medical disability that hinders his or her ability to complete the tasks of proper parenting. Each family member can be categorized with one of six basic roles, and the roles can change as people exit or enter the family unit.

It was initially difficult for me to identify my role within my family as I looked back over my childhood. Then I realized it was because my family makeup was always changing. I had lived with many different adults, and sometimes my siblings were with me and sometimes they were not. It made it difficult for me to know what part I was even playing within the household. As a young child, I definitely was the caretaker, also known as the enabler. I had to do my part to make sure everyone was going to be okay. I took on the identity of a mother when I realized that my mom was not equipped to do the job. The hero looks to make the family appear normal and tends to be a high achiever. The scapegoat or problem child is the one who takes the blame for the family dysfunction. Sometimes parents will place the blame for their poor decisions on that child:"I drink so much because I can't deal with how Jimmy behaves." The lost child is quiet and unseen. That child doesn't want to draw any attention and just tries to stay out of the way. I relate to this role as well. The mascot or class clown is the role that uses humor to divert attention away from the dysfunction. Masterminds use the opportunity of the family dysfunction to get it to work in their favor. An example of the mastermind is a child who sees that the parents are so consumed with their chaos, they won't notice if that child steals some money and takes the car for a joyride with no license.

One of my biggest takeaways from learning about family roles has been identifying why I felt I had to be a certain way growing up. It also allowed me to become more aware of things I do now as an adult. We often don't know why we are the way we are; we think we are just that way. Learning about the why empowers us to become free from beliefs that hold us back from healing and becoming our best selves. I started the journey of addressing my codependency during my teenage years. Today that codependency is referred to as "self-love deficit disorder." As much as I am not a fan of changing terminology (since it makes things confusing), I think this new term is fitting. It explains right in the name what the issue is: a self-love deficit. It also tells us what our end goal should be: to love ourselves. It has been crucial for me to learn healthy boundaries so I can care for myself. Boundaries help us not to get enmeshed with others and resort back to people pleasing.

The following chart is my version of the Dysfunctional Family Chart. I wanted to give a general overview of the roles, the internal struggles and the external behaviors that might be exhibited.

Role	What is going on inside	Coping mechanisms/ behaviors
Absent Parent (Addiction/Mental Health/Chronic Physical Ill Health)	• Shame, self-loathing, feeling of being unlovable, unforgiveness for self and others.	• Uses drugs/alcohol or other distractions to numb the pain.
Caretaker/Enabler	• Believes the absent parent needs him/her to survive. • "I have to be the parent; I have no choice."	• Is co-dependent, seeks approval, is people pleasing. • Focuses on keeping absent parent "happy" to keep everyone safe.
Scapegoat (Black sheep)/Problem Child	• Feels blamed for all the family's problems. • Feels he/she doesn't fit in (sometimes even looks physically different from rest of family).	• Seeks acceptance and validation. • Might shut down and cut people off. • Is rebellious as a child.
Mascot/Class Clown	• Learns to turn off emotions. • Wants people to believe nothing affects him/her. • Feels high stress and anxiety. • Has panic attacks, ulcers and other stress-related diseases.	• Is silly and mischievous. • Tries to make everything humorous to relieve tension in home. • Is unable to take things seriously as an adult as a result.
Hero/Golden Child	• Fears rejection and is afraid to say "no" (becomes a "yes" person). • Has very little sense of self. • Seeks to be perfect, obedient and attentive. • Has severe anxiety and depression.	• Academic overachievers. • Eating disorders or other control disorders. • Suicide ideation/nervous breakdowns. • "I have to be perfect to not cause any more problems for my family."
Mastermind	• Is highly intelligent. • Shuts down emotions to survive. • Feels justified in his/her behavior because of family situation.	• Subtly manipulates family situation to own advantage. • Narcissistic and sometimes even sociopathic behaviors. • Has social abilities to have people do what he/she wants.
The Lost Child	• Neglected. • Shame, mistrust. • Socially withdrawn, and shows low self-esteem.	• Invisible (either by choice or circumstance). • Introverted. • Doesn't speak much or show emotion. • May have serious health issues that go untreated for a long time.

Figure 3: Dysfunctional Family Roles Chart

7
Learning to Stand Alone

It was relatively early in my life when I concluded that no one was coming to save me. No one was going to stop the pain from happening. No one was going to stand with me and for me. In fact, as far as I could see, no one even saw me. Thus I stayed hidden for most of my early years of life, just observing the chaos. When that did not work and the pain got too significant, I started immersing myself in the chaos. I developed some attention-seeking habits, yet even those failed me. I started doing the very things I hated. A simple example is how I started smoking cigarettes. I hated that my dad smoked. When he would not quit, I started. I thought that if he saw me smoking and saw how he had negatively impacted me, then he would stop. Instead, my room was literally torn up. My dressers and mattresses were flipped over and practically destroyed. I was nine years old and looking for my dad to be a better role model. I was punished the first few times I was caught, but by the time I was 12, he was letting me smoke his cigarettes.

I believe attention-seeking behaviors in children are a huge indicator that something is off and needs to be addressed. The same is true for adults. Too often I have heard people say, "Oh, they're just looking for attention," and they dismiss or punish the individual. I am not saying these behaviors are the appropriate way of seeking help. However, many people are screaming, "Please see me; I'm not okay," when they act in these ways. As anyone reading this book can understand, it is hard sometimes to come up with the words to explain what is going on inside of us. It is hard to explain in words what we need or even know what we need. When our poor attempts at getting attention are dismissed, ignored or punished, it furthers our rejection. It leaves us feeling even more alone and believing that no one cares.

We develop this knowing that people are not safe, that they do not care, that it is up to us to care for ourselves. Some of us develop this belief very early in life. For me, I was only six years old when I realized I had to grow up and start taking care of myself because no one else was going to do it for me. It makes for a very lonely life, developing this mindset. It deems all people to be the same, yet leaves us craving relationships with others. It's painful trying to walk alone in this world. On the other hand, it can feel very safe, even peaceful, at times. If no one is there to hurt us, then no one can hurt us. Still, at the core of our being, we were created for relationships. God created us to have a relationship with Him. We cannot deny the yearning to be in relationships with others. Again, the tricky part is learning what safe people are and choosing those kinds of relationships.

We are only familiar with what is familiar. That is why hurt people gravitate to other hurt people and try to fix one another, only to cause more damage unintentionally. I had never seen a healthy family or marriage in my upbringing, so what was I using to gauge my relationships? Of course, I turned to television, movies and fantasy. My ideas were as farfetched as an animated movie that has a happily-ever-after ending. That leads to a lot of disappointment. This idea that someone else is going to come and make it all better leads us down a path of unmet expectations that then leads to bitterness toward others.

There are some very amazing people in this world. At the same time, it is not realistic to believe that someone is going to ride in on a white horse and save the damsel (you) in distress. Television shows and movies do young women a disservice by painting a false picture of what life will look like. Someone else is coming to save you. It makes people, especially women, vulnerable to toxic relationships because they go into those relationships with high unspoken expectations.

Have you ever tried to save someone in distress? You can do everything in your power to "fix" that person's life, and nothing changes. Why? It's because the person wants you to do all the work and not put any work into himself or herself. I understand because I have been on both sides many times. I have been the rescuer and I have been the victim, and I have failed at both. I failed because neither role allows you to find a place of contentment; both have within themselves a repeating cycle that never ends.

It is important for me to talk about the other side of this dilemma. Once we realize that no one is going to save us, we can become bitter. We feel rejected because the other person couldn't do what we needed that person to do. Without communication, without clear expectations and a sincere devotion to working together on the problem (instead of demanding someone else fix our issue), relationships fall apart. I remember going into relationships unknowingly expecting my significant other to "complete" me and make me whole. I would never say that, yet my reactions made it known.

After being let down again, I would grow bitter and resentful. I would start to separate myself mentally and emotionally from the relationship. In other words, I stayed in the relationship but was cold, hard and uncaring to the other person. That made sense to me; that is what I did with my mom when she abandoned me. Doing so protected me as a child, and it became my reaction to pain. Numbing pain became my number one survival instinct. It's called dissociation.

Dissociation is disconnecting from yourself and the world. This is a typical reaction for people who have endured trauma; they dissociate during the event(s). For individuals who have endured a lot of traumas, like me, it can become a comfortable response to go to whenever any stress happens. When people can no longer endure, they disconnect from themselves and the world in order to survive. I attribute my ability to dissociate as a huge reason I am alive today. I am not saying it is a healthy or wise way to survive trauma, but the alternative could be death.

I developed control issues as a result. There are so many things we cannot control in this life, and I became obsessed with controlling what I could. This is where my eating disorders developed. I could not control how my dad treated me or talked to me when I was a teen; however, I could decide if I would eat or if I would throw up my food. I would feel like I was in control of something. It gave me a fake sense of control over my life to decide how to treat food. When I would have hunger pangs and choose to starve myself, I would feel like I had power over the situation. When I would binge and purge, I would feel like I had control over my life. It was something *I* got to control. It was a completely false sense of control, and, in the process, I was damaging my physical body. But it took my attention from all the things that were happening around me. I became obsessed with what I did or did not eat.

It didn't lessen the effects of what was happening to me and around me; it was just giving me the façade that my life was completely manageable. I would later have to unpack all the damage done that I was unwilling and unable to face at the time. No matter what way people use to try to avoid dealing with their life problems, the problems will remain there until they are dealt with.

I fast regularly now; however, I do not do it to try to control my environment. There is a huge difference between fasting and starving yourself.

Starving yourself is self-abuse. I have gotten into a safe place now with my **body dysmorphia**, and I understand that I am a healthy weight. Like every other person in the world, I still have insecurities, but I don't allow them to dictate my daily activities anymore. Instead, I fast for two reasons. First, I fast for spiritual discipline. Fasting is an amazing way to build self-discipline/self-control, which is a fruit of the Spirit and draws us closer to God. For me, it has allowed me to hear God more clearly and have better supernatural discernment. The second reason I fast regularly is for the physical and health benefits.

As a person who has experienced significant physical trauma, my body has taken a beating over the years. My brain and body have experienced significant damage between stress, trauma, drug addiction, abuse and concussions. There is a lot of science out there now around the topic of fasting and its health benefits. It recycles and removes damaged cells. It also burns our stored fats, and unless you are just naturally slender, all people need help with burning excess fat.

In conclusion, it is normal when you have been abandoned or rejected in life to deem people as unsafe. It is also normal for you to try to control as much of your life as possible when things were out of control in your past. Even though these responses are normal, that does not make them healthy or acceptable, especially when you use isolation and control to such a degree that you do not enjoy moments of life. If you are unsure if you isolate, have attention-seeking behaviors or have control issues, consider asking yourself, when you are feeling out of sorts, "Why am I doing this, and is this helpful?" For example, for me, when I spend a day in bed, I have to check in with myself and ask, "Am I doing this because I'm exhausted and need rest, or am I doing this because I'm hurt and hiding from people?" Even if I am staying in bed because I am hurt, I will allow myself to rest for a period of time before making myself get back around my family and loved ones. Why? Because the enemy, the devil, loves to get you hyperfocused on your feelings, for then he can take you down a dark path of either selfishness or self-pity.

8
The Gathering

I titled this chapter "The Gathering" because that is exactly what I started doing with all the shame I was carrying around. As a young child, every time I saw or heard something that was crude or abusive, it made me feel "yucky." I was not the doer of the behaviors; however, I took on the humiliation of knowing it was not supposed to be that way. I was helpless in speaking up or doing anything about it. I was a young child, and it was the adults around me doing hideous things. They obviously had their own gathering of shame and rejection and acted recklessly to deal with their own brokenness. The lines get blurred in generational trauma and sin. The very thing children hate and despise can become part of their life to numb the pain they endured. It is such a normal part of their life in childhood that, if left undealt with, it becomes a part of their adulthood. It is often how victims become perpetrators. Children learn to perform so as to not rock the boat. For those who fight back, sometimes the damage done is worse.

I remember watching my brother fight back and being sincerely concerned that he was going to die. I screamed on multiple occasions, "Stop! You're going to kill him!" when I was just a young girl. I didn't fight back. For a long time, I didn't make waves. I gathered all of it inside, not letting any of it out. No one even knew I was screaming on the inside, all the time.

There are multiple ways a person responds to this buildup—probably even more than I am aware of. For me, the prominent responses were hopelessness and suicide ideation. I talk more extensively on that in my first book, *Why I Tried to Die*. Typically there is anger and bitterness toward those who hurt you, and eventually it comes out at everyone. This is also something I experienced.

Many things can develop out of survival, and all of them crack the soul and the **psyche**. Many dissociative, social and **mood disorders** can result. I will address some of these at the end of this chapter. My hope is that through learning about these disorders, you can better understand yourself and others with whom you may work or be in a relationship.

Now, I am not saying that everyone who has been diagnosed with one of these disorders has been abused as a child. From my experience and what I have learned, the root cause is usually unresolved trauma, whether that trauma was realized or not. Remember, any trauma is relative from one person to another. What one person deems as a traumatic event may not have been traumatic for another person.

In my life, I have gone through stages of response. The first ten years of my life, I tried to be the perfect child. When that buildup became too much, and I was not noticed or encouraged for my goodness, I ran. I learned to run away when things were not as they should be. That is when I bounced around a lot and eventually chose to be without a home as a teen. It felt safer to just be on my own. After my dad made me live with him, the trauma and shame that came with life there increased tenfold. With every new thing I had to endure, I started fracturing inside. Eventually I was unable to endure it anymore and had to start abusing substances myself to forget, even if just for a moment, what my everyday life was like.

I was just gathering all this pain and suffering and never speaking a word about it. The longer it stayed inside, the dirtier I felt. Shame is not simply being humiliated by our own actions; it is also being humiliated by what is being done to us. We cannot understand why it is happening. We want so desperately to understand why it is happening that we blame ourselves.

Every time I was abused in any way, I would replay the incident over and over in my head. I would change one thing that I said or did, and then play the rest of the story out in my mind. I was able to change the ending by doing this. The conclusion I pulled out from replaying the abuse was that it was my fault. If I had said or done that one thing differently, it would not have happened. As a result, I would feel that I was the one who was bad. Therefore, I would gather another layer of shame. *Do not believe the lie that it is your fault when someone hurts you.* You are only responsible for yourself and your actions, and you cannot cause someone to hurt you. It is definitely not your fault.

Between gathering all this rejection and shame, I was exhausted. All the little things become big things because I could not deal with the big things.

I dissociated from the big things; I blocked them out. I tried to make myself believe that they did not happen, that they were not real. But the little things…oh, I would snap about the little things.

By the time I started seriously dating (not childhood play), I was a mess. I felt so worthless and dirty that I could not see anything valuable about me. I also was so angry for the life I had been given. My outside appearance presented a confident, aggressive girl who took charge and did not let anyone push her around. I would get into fights just based on how someone would look at me! *Literally!* Internally, I was petrified that people would see just how dirty and worthless I was and treat me as such. I put myself in a lot of very dangerous situations, and it is only by the grace of God that I made it out of any of them.

Once I started choosing relationships in which I was treated badly, things became even harder. I did not choose my parents; none of us does. However, I did choose these relationships. I would play it cool and tough when I was first introduced to someone. Then, once I caught feelings for that person, I would invest my entire happiness and existence into that other person. Honestly, I would latch on for dear life. I would get attached in an unhealthy way. When I was treated poorly, I blamed myself. I allowed it. I tolerated it. I somehow set up allowances for me to be treated this way. I believed my worth was just that, to be treated like trash.

When I was treated poorly, it caused more shame and humiliation. I covered up for years what was happening in my first marriage. I did not want to see it myself, and I believed things could be different. I wore a mask so well that by the time I took the mask off, no one believed what I had been hiding. I lost a lot of key, important people in my life because of it. They just could not believe it. The thing is, I was so good at covering up secrets within a home because I had done it all my life. I had learned to wear a mask of "being happy" at a very early age. I was carrying the secrets of those around me and my own pain of what it was doing to me. I didn't even know who I was! I was what people wanted me to be.

I became what I thought I was supposed to be, what the world and others demanded of me. Sometimes the pressure would be too much. Then I would have a mental breakdown and end up self-medicating or staying in the hospital for a week. When I would get out, you guessed it: life was still there, waiting for me with its demands. Even while getting treatment for my mental health, I could not reveal all that was going on. I had to keep people's secrets. I had to protect people. No one was protecting me, yet I became a great secret keeper and protector at an early age. I'm still not sure how great I was at it.

Yes, people did not know the secrets, but they ate away at me like termites in the structure of a house. The foundation was becoming weak. My foundation was, in one sense, built on sand. If you are familiar with a foundation that has shifted, then you know it can cause great damage. Walls can crack, and floors can slant. The whole structure can be damaged and sometimes will cave in.

That was what was happening to me. My structure was becoming very weak and damaged. From the outside I looked like I had it together. However, if I let you inside and know about me, then you would see how weak and damaged I truly was. I think that for a long time I really believed someone would come along with a secret ingredient and fix it all. I got angry and bitter when no one did. It was like people had the key to life and were not sharing it with me.

When my marriage failed, and I got divorced, the shame nearly killed me. It broke me in a way that I did not even understand at the time. Anger took over. My mind and words were hateful and fueled with failure. At the same time, my heart was broken, and my soul exhausted. I tried my best to do what I always did, which was act like I was fine and move on. However, I started making reckless decisions based off my pain and exhaustion. I was not thinking with the logical part of my brain at all. I was fully living from my feelings.

When I became pregnant with someone else's baby while still legally married, I felt even more humiliated. I was in a bad situation, and it seemed that with every move I made, it kept getting worse. I realized I was living from my feelings and tried my best to go back and fix my marriage. Unfortunately, we both realized too much damage had been done. Now my mental and physical health were taking a beating. It was getting harder to keep it together and even have a good day. All this shame was becoming too much to bear.

During this same time, I had an accident and injured my head. I was working in the mental health field and was on the job at the time of injury. The floor was wet from the children after they played in the sprinkler, and I slipped and hit my head. I avoided getting assistance immediately because I had just found out that day that the child with whom I was working was experiencing abuse at home. Trauma to the brain, though, is brutal. I had no idea. I had no idea what had happened beyond my physical injury. Because the brain is the hub of our entire body, much can be damaged without there being any physical awareness. I did not realize that the logical part of my brain went on hiatus. (Even my brain did not want to be around! I would have left myself too, if I could.) Even with a CT scan, they cannot tell what is damaged in totality. There was indication of damage through the physical problems: a posture tremor, seizures, lack of mobility, fatigue and so forth. It was as if my physical appearance was starting to reflect my emotional state. I was frail and brittle-looking. I was 28 years old when this happened, yet I had the physical and emotional strength of someone at the end of life. Or at least, that is how I felt. On the doctor's recommendation, I became "permanently disabled."

All of this I blamed myself for. I was not doing anything bad when I got injured; I was working in the mental health field with children in need. I thought it was the right thing to do to stay at work longer than I should have to help the child I was working with. I honestly just believed that I was destined to have this life of bad things happening to me, and there was nothing I could do about it. My heart was always for people, yet people never seemed to have a heart for me. That's what I believed. Those who did care did not stick in my memory. I only remembered those who hurt me—all those people's faces in my memory yelling that I was no good, that it was my fault that they were no good to me, that it was what I deserved.

Around this time I lost myself altogether. I vaguely looked like the person I used to be. The shame and rejection and hopelessness that came with the injury became too much, and I threw in the towel. My morals and values diminished. They did not seem to have a place anymore within my life. I could not even tell you what a boundary was at that point. I felt that I would not make it if I did not become like those around me. And *that*, my friend, is one of the biggest lies of all. But I believed it. I completely lost myself. Today when I recall where I was mentally at that time, it is painful. I want to go back and hug the me of that time and say, "You can do it a different way. You are so loved." Unfortunately, I cannot do that. What I can do is use what I learned about what almost took me out and help as many others as possible. So, I am saying to you, *you can do it a different way*. Do not sell yourself short, give in to this world's demands, and compromise who you are.

I was not aware that we can only serve one master. I did not know that if we are not serving God, then we are consciously or unconsciously serving satan. I can see now in hindsight what unfolded. At the time I thought I was only doing what I could for my life not to get worse. However, just like Eve in the garden, I was deceived. I believed that I could make my life better for my children and me if I became like the world. Like the saying goes, if you cannot beat them, join them. I tried my whole life to be this person everyone wanted me to be (at least I thought so), and it left me all but dead. I was so tired of being the victim. I was so sick of being the damsel in distress and no one showing up to save me. I tried doing it the right way. But I did not have the strength to keep fighting.

Shame and rejection became my two best friends. They were always there for me. They kept me comfortable because they were so familiar to me. I got to the point where I could not leave my house during the day. I could not let people see me. I could not pretend to be okay anymore. I could not put on a mask and go out and be the life of the party or even walk down to the corner store. I just enjoyed staying in my sweet misery by myself, in the torment of my life, my living hell.

People would tell me that suicide was a sin and I would go to hell. I already was living in hell every day. My life was tortuous, and I felt it could not get any worse. Scaring people into the kingdom of God does not work in today's age. Some people live in hell in their daily life now.

Our brains are powerful, and we can do magnificent things to keep ourselves alive. At my breaking point in 2013, I split into two separate persons altogether to make it through alive. I believe I developed a split personality or **dissociative identity disorder** to survive the level of stress and trauma I was experiencing. I do not remember large blocks of my life during this time. I had different names. My physical appearance, voice and personality would change when I was this other person. It was as if the part of me that wore a mask had split into a different person inside of me to protect me and keep me alive while doing things I could not endure doing.

Going Deeper

I have mentioned dissociating a few times throughout this book. It is important to define and explain it. Again, dissociation is disconnecting from reality to survive when our brain can no longer endure what it is going through. The brain goes into overload and basically takes the stance that it must shut down. There are a handful of diagnoses that involve dissociating, and they are the result of either stressful or traumatic events. Psychiatrists might throw blanket diagnoses on an individual and overlook or lump these specific disorders into other diagnoses such a **posttraumatic stress disorder** (PTSD) or borderline personality disorder. (I will cover PTSD in a different chapter.)

There are five core symptoms that help identify these dissociation disorders. An individual can have one or all of the following: **amnesia, depersonalization,** derealization, **identity confusion** and identity alteration ("DSM-5 Dissociative Disorders"). People typically associate amnesia with hitting their head and forgetting who they are; however, people can have amnesia or gaps in memory for psychological reasons. These gaps can vary in time from minutes to years. That is why I say that I don't remember a large block of time from 2012 to 2014. The images in my memory are spotty, and I question whether they happened or not. Some of this memory loss was due to the aftereffects of my brain injury, but mostly I believe it was due to stress. *Depersonalization* is disconnecting from oneself. Sometimes this happens when individuals self-harm so as to try to feel real again. *Derealization* is disconnecting from people and things that should be familiar to the individual. *Identity confusion* is just as it states, a confusion about one's identity. And identity alteration is what I believe I experienced in 2013 when I became different personalities. During this altered state, people can use different names, lose time and learn things they don't remember learning.

9
My Idols

An idol is an image or representation of a god that is used as an object of worship. It also is a person or thing that is greatly admired, loved or revered. Because of my lack of love for myself, because of my self-hatred, I latched onto things and people. I *needed* them to just get by. They were my security. Cigarettes, pills, men, my anger, my self-pity and even my children—I was obsessed with them all. I didn't know how to get by without them. Even my physical body would respond in withdrawal when I didn't have them. They felt essential. They were my gods. I adored and worshiped these people and things, and the idolization was suffocating me.

I had to take a break for a year from my writing. I started getting attacked hard with adversity (difficulties), and it was too much for me. God revealed to me that I needed to go deeper into my healing before I could continue with writing. Obviously, satan gets angry any time I speak because I am always glorifying God and revealing the lies and tactics of the enemy. Since I was writing about unraveling shame and rejection for this book, he decided to throw many of those very real situations at me.

For example, one thing that happened was someone from my past coming back around. He didn't come back directly into my life; rather, he moved near the home of one of my safest couples. In a very nonchalant, innocent way, my husband let me know that my ex had moved near my pastor. I was like, "Huh? What, who, where, why?!" My husband really didn't understand what was going on inside of me as I felt triggered, and the walls grew tight around me as I started to panic.

If you have read my first book, *Why I Tried to Die*, you need to know that I didn't even bring up this relationship in that book. This particular relationship happened after my relationships with Jay and Kurt. It came about after

I was so battered and bruised emotionally and physically, when I was but a shell of a person. Let's call this man Sean. When I met Sean, which happened to be on his birthday, I lived as my dissociated self. He didn't meet Lisa. He met Alexis, Natalie or Winter, my three alter personas that had emerged to keep me alive. Sean met a fun, "high as a kite but living on an emotional roller coaster" girl. Sean was one of the three people whom I shared about in my first book robbing me upstairs while I was downstairs getting interviewed by a detective. What I didn't explain in the book was that I knew Sean was using me. He was ten years younger than me, and I was permanently disabled and on bed rest. What would he want from me?! Well, I had money, an apartment and a car, for starters, and he had none of that. I always had weed and pills and was always available to "turn up." Once I got enough drugs in me, I forgot how sick I was, and then we would go to the after-hours clubs and party until the sun came up. When he would get jammed up with the law, I would put money on his books, phone and pay off his dockets to get him out of jail early, and get probation off his back.

One of the most painful things I experienced in that relationship was the moment he found out that I was paying for everything with the money I made from escorting. (Well, my man, I'm permanently disabled and living off Social Security Disability Insurance, making $772 a month. Where do you think it's coming from?!) We were at his mom's house when he found out that I was escorting. I was in bed even at her place because my depression and physical health were so bad that I could not function. He came into her bedroom and asked me straight out, and I told him the truth. He spit in my eye. Right into my eye! Here I am barely holding on to life, prostituting myself to take care of a grown man, and he spits in my eye when he finds out that I was getting that money by selling myself? "Thank you" would have been sufficient! I jumped up, freaking out, and tried to harm myself right there on the spot. Sean and his cousin took me to the Emergency Room and dropped me off. I somehow was able to talk myself out of being hospitalized that day, but I came home to my place and was not okay. My thoughts day and night were on death. This happened around the same time my children were taken by their dad. It was at that point when I counted out 300 opiate pills and tried again to take my life.

Parts of this time were still too shameful for me to reveal in my first book. Since this book is about learning to reveal and unravel shame, I must be honest about the things I don't want to remember. I must be honest that I held up this man as an idol, as a god, while he couldn't have cared whether I lived or died. What happened when he met my pastor proved that point. His then-girlfriend stated to my pastor that she worked in reentry, which made my pastor say, "Oh, then do you know Lisa Kessler-Peters?" Sean responded with, "Oh, I know her. I used to go with her before she got into that lifestyle she was in and got arrested!" What he won't admit, and that is fine, is that he played a large part in my getting into that lifestyle. When all of this happened, I had already made peace with who I used to be, but it was his coming into what I felt was my safe space that made me uncomfortable. It was like I couldn't visit my pastor's home anymore because my safe space had been tampered with.

An interesting fact is that all three people who were part of stealing my $2,000 that I needed for my Jeep found themselves also at the county jail while I was there. I didn't need to get back at them for what they did to me; their lifestyle took care of that without my doing anything. It's so easy to ask why you would allow someone to treat you that way. I asked myself the same question. The answer is that it is what I believed I deserved. I didn't realize that I was getting treated that way because I allowed it. I know that women today believe chivalry is dead and men are no longer kind and loving, so we must settle for less. No! Men are still chivalrous and kind, but if we keep accepting juvenile behavior instead of that of grown men, they will continue to act like juveniles! If we keep parenting men instead of being partners, this behavior is what we will get.

My husband is kind and gentle. And even though he is one of a kind, he is not the only man like this left in the world. My David knows everything about me, and he never uses my past to hurt or harm or take advantage of me. I treat him with that same kindness. I thought for sure I would have to "settle" due to what I had gone through and what I had done to myself. I felt as if I was used goods and that there was not a "best" out there for me as an option. I guess I never believed that was an option for me, even before all that I went through. I was just looking for anyone who would accept my broken self before Jesus came into my life and showed me just how precious and beautiful I was. You are that same kind of precious and beautiful. Don't allow people to use you and take advantage of you. Set the tone for how you will be treated, and you don't have to be a jerk about it, either. You can keep it classy, ladies and gentlemen.

Idols—whether people or things—pull on our emotions. An idol will never fully satisfy us, but we will focus on it as if it is the beginning and end of everything. We will allow the weight of these emotions to take us out of character and become someone else if we are not careful. Once I met Jesus, everything changed. He is the one who should truly hold that place. The best part is, He truly does satisfy. Scripture is full of evidence; Jesus is the answer.

I am convinced that my God will fully satisfy every need you have, for I have seen the abundant riches of glory revealed to me through Jesus Christ! (Philippians 4:19 TPT)

Concerning food sacrificed as offerings to idols, we all know that an idol is nothing, for there is no God but one (1 Corinthians 8:4 TPT).

Shame covers all who boast in other gods, for they worship idols. For all the supernatural powers once worshiped the true and living God. But God's Zion-people are content, for they know and hear the truth… (Psalm 97:7–8 TPT).

They began to serve their gods and bow before their idols. All of this led them away from you and brought about their downfall (Psalm 106:36 TPT).

Even though you were once distant from him, living in the shadows of your evil thoughts and actions, he reconnected you back to himself. He released his supernatural peace to you through the sacrifice of his own body as the sin-payment on your behalf so that you would dwell in his presence. And now there is nothing between you and Father God, for he sees you as holy, flawless, and restored. If indeed you continue to advance in faith, assured of a firm foundation to grow upon. Never be shaken from the hope of the gospel you have believed in. And this is the glorious news I preach all over the world (Colossians 1:21–23 TPT).

10
Ouch, That Hurt

Another happening that caused me to stop writing was finding out that my father was at the end of his life. At the end of my first book, I stated that my father was going to walk me down the aisle on my wedding day. That never got to happen. Unfortunately, my father started getting very sick and had to stop working, which meant he ended up not having a vehicle. Due to the COVID-19 pandemic, the doctors kept pushing out his surgeries and appointments while the hospitals kept releasing him home because they were so overcrowded with life-sustaining situations and didn't consider my father's situation to be life-threatening. On top of the lack of medical care my father received, he also was self-medicating with the thing he always had used in the past: alcohol. He tried his best to make it to my wedding; he cried as he told me that he wasn't going to make it. He told me on his deathbed that of all the things he missed in my life, missing my wedding made him the saddest.

Then, in August 2021, my father dropped his remote and, when he went down to get it, could not get up off the floor. He thought he broke his back. The hospital did scans and found that it was cancer, and it was too far progressed for the doctors to really be able to do anything about it. My father refused treatment because he knew he wouldn't be able to make a full recovery and didn't want to spend the end of his life in tremendous pain from the treatment.

When I received the text from my brother that my dad was in the hospital and that it didn't look good, I turned my phone over and continued working. I was in shock. If I didn't say it out loud, would it be true? I worked on vendor-event materials for two more hours late into the night before stopping. When I went to bed, my husband was already there, and I said something snarky to his gentle, embracing words. He asked me what that was about, and I lost my whole mind. I started crying inconsolably. I became enraged that I was never going to get the restored relationship with my dad that I so deeply wanted. When my dad accepted Jesus in 2019, it was the biggest miracle I ever experienced besides my own miracles. I had high hopes of being able to have a healthy relationship with my father—one that I was never able to have as a child. I wanted my children to have a grandfather whom I felt was safe for them to be around. I never had that before 2019.

For my whole life, my father was a toxic, unhealthy and twisted man. I experienced great neglect, abuse and loss of innocence at the hands of my father. Most of my trauma was directly related to my father's behaviors and actions or lack thereof. Most of my desire to commit suicide my entire life was because of the pain I carried that was associated with my father. I loved him, and he hurt me, a lot, repeatedly. He did not protect me. He caused harm to me, and I was his child. He was the bad guy in my "Lifetime movie." Even today I still suffer with symptoms of posttraumatic stress disorder, or PTSD.

Perhaps you have a person or people in your life whom you feel this same pain about. You may be wondering, "How did she learn to forgive the unforgivable?"

Going Deeper

As stated earlier, posttraumatic stress disorder (PTSD) and trauma are now being looked at a lot more closely. Trauma-informed care is talked about a lot in all social work fields. This trauma has existed the whole time, but the research and knowledge getting out to the community has increased in recent years. There is more than one type of PTSD. Suffering multiple traumas over long periods of time is known as complex PTSD. Another is minor trauma that may or may not affect a person for a long period of time. Unfortunately, I think one of the biggest hindrances to healing PTSD is that the medical field gives a diagnosis without attaching the hope that a "normal" life can still be obtained.

In my own experience, getting a mental health diagnosis only made me feel hopeless. It made me feel like I was permanently broken, and nothing could be done about it. I *became* my mental illness. It became my identity, and that was even with me as a professional with a degree working in the mental health field! Sometimes we cannot see our own stuff that we deal with internally. Even as a professional, for years I could not identify and cope with my trauma. Today I have learned to separate the symptoms of my mental health diagnosis from who I am. For example, I state that I am a person who deals with the symptoms of PTSD. That separates me and who I am from the symptoms of PTSD that I have to deal with. This works with any diagnosis, whether it be for mental health or physical health.

Some symptoms of PTSD include flashbacks and nightmares/night terrors, hypervigilance, avoidance of trauma triggers and emotionally numbing oneself. Trauma triggers can be sounds, sights, smells, places and people who remind the person of the trauma. A person can keep re-experiencing an event days, months, years and even decades after it happened ("Posttraumatic Stress Disorder [PTSD]" 2014). This causes hypervigilance, where the brain believes the event is happening again and will go into flight, fight or freeze mode even when nothing life-threatening is happening.

Here is a breakdown of the three responses: *flight* refers to running away; *fight* means you get reactive and want to defend yourself verbally or physically; and *freeze* simply means you can't move or respond in any way. With freeze you just shut down. Your adrenaline goes into action when your heart rate and blood flow increase and pain perceptions decrease. The flight, fight or freeze responses are the way your body protects itself in dangerous situations. The problem with the hypervigilance of PTSD is that your body will continue to resort to these responses even when you are no longer in danger.

Basically, we have to train our brain that it is safe and that danger is no longer present. I use self-regulation and grounding to do this for myself. First I acknowledge what I am feeling and try to identify why. Then I do something to change my atmosphere. I tell myself that I am okay and that I am not in danger. I take a drink or eat a bite of something to start to use my senses for other things to make my brain focus on those. I will get up and go for a walk or change my physical location in some way. I sometimes will rub my hands together. Doing these little mindfulness techniques helps to break the panic. These techniques help me to be responsive as opposed to reactive in situations. Reactivity puts us in panic mode, in which we are unable to control our behaviors and words. Responsiveness allows us to have a planned response from a level-minded place that does not require regretting the things we do and speak. This takes practice, but it becomes easier over time. Sometimes, with PTSD, a person experiences anger outbursts, irritability and/or self-destructive behaviors. Self-regulation can help with these, as well.

11
Forgiving the Unforgivable

How does a person get to this place? As humans we struggle with forgiveness. I don't think there are any true masters on the topic, because when we are hurt it seems impossible to forgive. It seems dangerous to forgive. Sometimes we feel like if we forgive, people won't have to pay for what they did to us. And they *must* pay! Someone must pay for this pain we are carrying around inside of us. *It is their fault, and they need to fix it!* Well, my friend, life doesn't work that way. So what do we do? We build walls—walls so high that no one can get in, and we can't get out. We build ourselves a prison. Yes, it's true. We put ourselves in prison and think that it is somehow going to get us the results that we ultimately desire. We isolate ourselves, then we feel further rejected and wonder why we are alone.

We humans are so silly. We desire connection and love and then push people away. We do not share what has hurt us or that we are hurt, yet we wait for someone to apologize. Unspoken expectations always come with a hefty cost because they always fall short. We will be let down *every single time!* We cannot read each other's minds. We end up disappointed. However, there is a simple fix, although it does take some courage. Simply say, "My feelings were hurt" and the reason why. Doing this gives us a better chance of getting some relief because we made our feelings known. The problem comes when we put conditions on what we need the other person's response to be.

I can say from experience that stating your feelings is difficult to learn to do when you never felt heard as a child, yet it is still doable. My childhood is the reason I struggled so much with sharing how I felt. No one seemed to care when I was hurt as a child, so I learned to stop sharing. I bottled it all in until I imploded or exploded. That didn't help either. I would be reactive instead of responsive to the things that were hurting me because, by the time

I said something, I had exploded like a bomb—screaming, fighting, throwing things. Yes, that happens when you hold in pain. I was unable to reveal what was really going on because it looked like anger when it actually was disappointment, loneliness, sadness, fear, betrayal, bitterness or insecurity, to name a few. Anger is a large emotion that covers up other feelings. Why? Because it's safer.

Putting conditions on forgiveness is not a good choice either. Having boundaries and standards for whether you stay in a relationship with someone based on that person's response, on the other hand, is a good choice. A simple example is when your boyfriend (or girlfriend) knows that his/her actions or words hurt you, but blames you for what he/she did. If he says, "You made me cheat on you because you didn't talk to me for two days," then it indicates that you need to stop having a relationship with him. Should you forgive the other person? Yes. Why? Because it releases you from the toxic chemicals you are holding in your body by not forgiving. Do you keep having a relationship with that person? No. Why? Because the individual is not remorseful or taking accountability for his or her part in what happened. In not forgiving the person, you are still engaged in a relationship with him or her emotionally and mentally. Because your thoughts and feelings are still associated with the traumatic event, the same toxins will continue to be released. In forgiveness, you are freeing yourself from the emotional and mental attachment and from the toxins they produce. Ultimately, you are responsible for your feelings.

You and I don't get to say, "They made me angry!" Yes, other people might have caused you to react with anger, but you chose to feel that emotion. I know for certain that if someone had tried to explain to me a decade or two ago that I was responsible for my anger, I would have become angry. I would have disagreed and held firm to my belief that "they made me feel that way." There is research today that shows that you can identify your feeling as it is happening and choose to not stay fixated on it. Biblically there is a lot of truth to this statement, as well.

> We can demolish every deceptive fantasy that opposes God and break through every arrogant attitude that is raised up in defiance of the true knowledge of God. We capture, like prisoners of war, every thought and insist that it bow in obedience to the Anointed One. Since we are armed with such dynamic weaponry, we stand ready to punish any trace of rebellion, as soon as you choose complete obedience (2 Corinthians 10:5–6 TPT).

That is powerful! When you choose obedience to God, you have the authority to control your feelings. Reading that either made you super excited or very annoyed because you now cannot "unknow" that information. You are welcome. So, if you choose to do nothing with it, then you are choosing disobedience to the Word of God.

When I came to this understanding, I had to do something about it. I was so hungry for the Word of God that when I read something like this scripture, I would pray with faith that I would be able to do it. Then I would act in accordance with that word. At first it was a lot harder than it is now. Obviously, when we have been doing things one way our whole life, it is very difficult to start doing them a different way. However, one of the most amazing things about the Holy Spirit is that He helps us. He lives inside of us once we accept Jesus Christ as our Lord and Savior and ask the Holy Spirit to come live inside of us. He will lead us, and we just have to follow. That leading could be a little gentle prompting like, "Hey now, you don't talk like that anymore. You are a child of God." Keep in mind that we have free will. The Holy Spirit will not force us to do anything, so if we choose to go against His prompting, that's on us. He won't be angry with us, but it is for our benefit to listen to Him. (Unfortunately, there also is a way to quench the Holy Spirit. I won't get too deeply into that here.) I do believe that the Holy Spirit is always speaking, but if we aren't listening, we will not hear Him.

12
Hide Those Animals

R ecently I attended the annual retreat for advisory council and board members for the Pennsylvania Prison Society and was reminded of a very pressing pain that I felt during my incarceration—that the incarcerated are the invisible population in our society. They are the voiceless and faceless population; they are the oppressed, the rejected, the ones thrown away.

I remember, during my arrest, trying to explain what had happened in response to what they stated they were charging me with. It was then that I realized it did not matter what I said; they had already concluded what they believed had occurred and ripped my voice right from my mouth. It was the familiar pain of not being heard. It was the reason I stopped talking in the first place as a child. No one would ever listen. No one cared. These officers looked at me like I was an animal, an offender, a bad person, and they responded accordingly. You can fight the justice system all you want, but without a support system and a lot of money, you are guilty without it being proven. I have had correctional officers yell at me to look at the floor. I've been told in an elevator at the courthouse to turn around and face the wall while being shackled and handcuffed. I've been screamed at and laughed at by correctional officers while crying and having panic attacks.

I remember feeling like that the horrible smell and the filthy conditions of the prison were becoming part of who I was. I was dirty and unable to get clean. No matter how hard I scrubbed in the shower, the filth wouldn't come off me. It went deeper than my skin. *It was all that familiar shame.* I was damaged and beyond repair. There was no coming back from this. Time inside was it for me. You are told when to get up and when to go to sleep. You are told when you can eat, shower, work, make phone calls, visit and go to meetings. If you even looked at the guards in a way they didn't like, it could all be ripped from you. You could be woken up from sleep to yelling and cells being tossed and being told to strip down and bend and cough. You could be locked down for a week at a time and restricted to your bunk bed. That meant no movement at all, even within your cell when on lockdown. You had to stay on your bed. This lockdown could simply be because they didn't have enough staff. Incarceration caused me to be always on edge. An inmate never knew what was going to happen. This is a traumatic way of living. It was similar to the pain of not knowing how my dad was going to act when he got drunk.

That fear followed me when I left the prison. My first night out of prison I couldn't even lie down to sleep. I had to sit up because I needed to be ready in case something happened. Whether I was driving down the street, walking through a grocery store, or just sitting at the library reading a book, there was an ever-present fear that they could come in, get me at any time, and take me back to jail. It is hard to move forward in life with this extreme amount of fear. I was unable to work or do much of anything at first. Even making phone calls was overwhelming.

Doors unexpectedly opening or closing startled me. Hearing keys jingle or anything metal clanking caused me to get ready, something bad might happen. This is hypervigilance due to trauma. How was I ever going to become a productive member of society? I was afraid of my own shadow.

Prison is set up to break you. But what does that do? How does that help rehabilitate someone? I see individuals who complete shorter sentences in prison come out one of two ways: broken or angry. Neither helps to create productive humans who can get their life together. I say "shorter sentences" because I believe people who finish longer sentences in prison have time to process all those feelings and come to accept accountability and move forward. There are exceptions, but these are my observations. At the same time, individuals who have longer sentences are so isolated from the world that they often don't know how to reacclimate themselves when they get out. They feel lost. They feel like outsiders.

The "super predators," as criminologist and political scientist John J. Dilulio Jr. in the 1990s called them, were juveniles who committed or were involved in a violent crime and had no remorse (Vitale 2018). This terminology basically says that these kids are dangerous and permanently no good, so let's toss them away. Those "super predators" from the 1990s are now in their later years of life and are some of the gentlest humans in the world. Once their brains fully developed, as psychology now shows happens around 25 years old, these individuals matured and had very few acting-out behaviors, even inside prison with life sentences.

However, the system considered it too late for these offenders (also known as children). People cried out that they were too dangerous, so these children were sentenced to life without parole as young as 12 years old. Do you know a 12- or 15-year-old whom you love and care for? Think about that young teen making a split decision that was a huge mistake and resulted in him or her spending the rest of his or her life in prison. Do you think that young person should ever be considered for release?

Thank God, a ruling in 2012 by the United States Supreme Court in *Miller v. Alabama* found that it was unconstitutional to sentence a juvenile offender to mandatory life without parole. In 2016 the United State Supreme Court made the ruling that *Miller* should be retroactively applied. What this did was allow juvenile lifers to seek out resentencing. In Pennsylvania, 482 lifers were resentenced and 281 have been released. I have come to know some of these individuals, and two of them I even call brothers.

A new study conducted by Montclair State University researchers has found a recidivism rate (defined as reconviction for any offense) of just 1.14% among people who were sentenced as juveniles in Philadelphia to life without the possibility of parole and then subsequently released. This is consistent with a growing body of scientific research that shows people age out of criminal behaviors, that lengthy sentences fail to deter crime, and that lengthy prison terms both divert funds from public health and safety initiatives and are counterproductive to strengthening families and communities (Philadelphia DAO 2020).

I would like to share the experiences of one of these individuals. He would like to remain anonymous, so I will refer to him as my "brother from a different mother with the same heavenly Father." This man is so very dear to me and has impacted my life in a huge way. The world deemed him an untreatable predator at the age of 16, locking him up and throwing away the key. The Lord, however, kept that key, and in His perfect timing, released him. He is the gentlest and kindest soul you would ever meet—nothing dangerous or predator-like about him. I would trust him in my home with my children (the most precious things to me) and with my finances and my friendship. As you should know by now, I do not trust others well. The following chapter is his story. As you read what he has to say and the poems he has written, think about this: Who are we locking up and throwing away the key to?

13
Forty-Two Years

Written by "My Brother," a Former Lifer
I was living a life of darkness at 16, one that led to my ultimate incarceration for 42 years. Many people seem to think there is no redemption, that men and women cannot change. That lie is perpetuated by our politicians. The Republican playbook is written with that fear in mind to win over those who live their lives in fear. I, among many others, serve as an example that people can change. Change is possible, but it cannot be achieved alone. God found me in my darkest place and brought me to my senses. Our society is said to be a Christian society, yet there is no forgiveness for the sinner. Throughout the Bible, there are stories of God's forgiveness. From the Old Testament into the New, God forgave mankind for his shortcomings. I once heard a preacher say, "Love the sinner, hate the sin." That's what we are called to do; we are to love our enemies and exhibit compassion towards others. As a society we are at a crossroads, and the question is, does a man like me deserve hope and opportunity?

My life has changed, as have I, but I didn't make the conversion alone. God sent people into my life to speak change and help me to change. My wife and friends are the tools used by God. When man said no, God said yes. I sit here writing this because of God and His work in me. I appreciate this opportunity to share my story in this book. My story is likened to that of Jonah's. I ran from God; I refused to do what He had called me to do. As a result, I ended up in the belly of the whale called "prison" until I humbled myself and cried out to God. He heard me. I can't tell my entire story in this setting, but hopefully through the following few poems you will get a picture of what my life was.

This Walk

The path before me is long and winding.
The road behind is chipped, shattered and broken.
How do I navigate this path?
How do I walk this road without reflecting?
Forty-two years, millions of tears, an exit of cheers,
A Brother on my left,
A Brother on my right.
We walked together in this long fight.
This walk is about you,
This walk is about me,
This walk is about the women and men you do not see.
My brothers from a different mother,
They educated me and lifted me up when the system put me down.
Forty-two years we walked,
Forty-two years we talked.
Forty-two years we shared our pain,
Forty-two years we fought to stay sane.
The gates opened for me,
But, what about my brothers?
When will the gates open for them?
When will we again share this walk?

Where Do I Run?

When the winds of life come pushing in, and my life is blown to pieces,
My head spins in circles, my heart races with fear.
Where do I run to?
I run to God, who shelters me and lifts me up.
He calms my fears and stills life's storms.
Where do I run to?
When life is tearing me down, and its trials beat me to the ground,
When my mind is confused and my way uncertain,
Where do I run to?
I run straight to God, who shelters me in His bosom
And wards off life's poisonous darts.
He clears my mind as He does the skies
And helps me to find answers and reasons why.
Where do I run to?

When I'm lost with nowhere to go,
No friends to laugh with,
No wife to hold,
Where do I run to?
To God, the only place that's safe from all the trials and struggles of life.

For Years
When I was 16, you turned and left me,
Standing in fear surrounded by darkness with very little HOPE.
I was not one to show my emotions,
So I cried inside, smiled in place of my fears.
I came to you seeking your love and protection,
Extending my hand for your grip of assurance.
But instead of that you pushed me away as if I never existed.
I fought this battle alone,
Receiving everlasting wounds.
My heart was filled with pain and sorrow,
But my greatest wound was the loss of you,
At the moment when I most needed you!
I struggled to find my inner strength,
Only to be weakened by self-sorrow.
I searched to find reasoning for your lack of understanding,
It did not exist…
I was forced to become a man at 16,
When I really didn't have a chance to grow.
I stood in a courtroom without your support or concern.
If I had had the strength I never would have cried,
But you drained me of what little strength I had,
And made me not care if I won or lost.
Because I felt I had already lost the most important thing in my life,
Which was you, but I hadn't.
Because the most important thing in life is life,
Which I lost without your ever knowing.
One day you will come to see the great pain that you've caused me.
But don't let it stop you from being you.
And don't say what you should have done.
Just thank God for opening both our eyes
Through the years.

14
Unclean

Have you ever felt unclean? Have you ever felt like you needed to get out of your own skin or to run away from yourself because you were just so disgusted by yourself? Have you done things or had things done to you that you have never said out loud, that cause you to quickly look away when you catch a glimpse of yourself in the mirror because you can't stand the sight of yourself? Not even your spouse or best friend knows it all, or at least how much it still hurts. That is shame.

I remember when I first learned about leprosy in the Bible and how people treated lepers. I felt like those lepers. Culturally, in biblical times, a person would be considered unclean from just being in contact with someone who had leprosy. As a culture, we, too, treat people this way. We avoid people whom we think of as unclean: the homeless, the addicts, the girls who had abortions, the prisoners or those released from prison. One morning while I was driving to work in Harrisburg, I looked up at the Capitol building and asked Jesus what rallies and protests at the Capitol He would be at if He still walked the earth.

I struggle with these issues because I know enough of God's heart to realize that we grieve Him so often with our fighting and division. Jesus replied to my question that morning, "I'd be at them all." He then proceeded to give me a vision of His sitting on the bottom steps of the Capitol. He said, "I love them all. I love the baby who died due to abortion, and I love the mother who felt like she had no choice. I love the individual sentenced to life in prison for murder, and I love the victim who died and their family members who are grieving. I cannot hold a sign that says one person's life is more important than another's, because all human life is made in the image of God and is precious. I don't live by law, but by mercy, grace, forgiveness and free will. I would attend all the rallies, and I would sit and wait for those who wanted to know about a new life, the life I give." And then He just smiled at me.

The answer is love. We would fix so many of the issues we struggle with within our society if we just loved people. Oh, we can be such pompous idiots. We fill our lives with distractions and opinions of others while we struggle with our own issues and insecurities. We think that if we compare ourselves with others who seemingly are doing a worse job of keeping it together, then we can throw stones. "What's wrong with *them*? Oh my goodness, they are so disgusting, how can anyone live that way?! I would never!" I think our very judgmental mouths and thoughts are why God always is having to humble us by allowing us to go through some things. We can be so puffed up on our high horses of superiority. We only have compassion for what we have gone through and struggle to hear the stories of others with different experiences and how those experiences made them into who they became.

What is the thorn in your side? What is an ongoing hardship for you? I have a thorn so sharp that at times I feel I cannot withstand it. Can anyone relate? Then I remember what Paul shares:

> The extraordinary level of the revelations I've received is no reason for anyone to exalt me. For this is why a thorn in my flesh was given to me, the Adversary's messenger sent to harass me, keeping me from becoming arrogant. Three times I pleaded with the Lord to relieve me of this. But he answered me, "My grace is always more than enough for you, and my power finds its full expression through your weakness." So I will celebrate my weaknesses, for when I'm weak I sense more deeply the mighty power of Christ living in me. So I'm not defeated by my weakness, but delighted! For when I feel my weakness and endure mistreatment—when I'm surrounded with troubles on every side and face persecution because of my love for Christ—I am made yet stronger. For my weakness becomes a portal to God's power (2 Corinthians 12:7–10 TPT).

This can be a difficult one, but let us get honest with ourselves. If everything in our life was perfect, would we even need God? Would the smoothness of our existence here on Earth somehow make us forget altogether that we are here on a mission? Would we maybe never even come to the realization that a God exists and that life on Earth is just part of our existence? I know people who do not believe God exists, and they live a YOLO (you only live once) lifestyle. It is painful to watch because they bring destruction and chaos into their own lives and then wonder why their lives are like that. I know because I did the same thing.

As a child, I did not choose for my purity to be taken from me, yet it was taken. The choice was not mine at any point. Once I believed that sex was my worth, I tried to use it as a weapon for my own gain. I learned from pornographic material, hearing people speak crudely, seeing people act in a crude manner, and being in environments where sex was promoted in a vulgar and crass way. I learned from music that, for decades now, promotes sex as a raunchy, vulgar power trip—music played over the radio and pushed especially onto younger children and teens. We may think nothing of it. We often do not even think about it; We have a "it's just the way it is" kind of mentality. What it is doing and continues to do, though, is promote generations of sexual perversions that have been around for centuries.

Sexuality is not a bad thing. Sex was never intended to be a smutty, naughty, sleazy thing. Sexuality was created by God. Some will even argue that the first sin was the distortion of sexuality, not eating actual fruit. However, the first sin was disobedience to God—to hear God tell you exactly what to do and not do, then decide to go and try the very thing He instructed you not to do. Genesis 1, the very beginning of the Bible, explains it clearly:

> God spoke: "Let us make human beings in our image, make them reflecting our nature so they can be responsible for the fish in the sea, the birds in the air, the cattle, and, yes, Earth itself, and every animal that moves on the face of Earth." God created human beings; he created them godlike, reflecting God's nature. He created them male and female. God blessed them: "Prosper! Reproduce! Fill Earth! Take charge! Be responsible for fish in the sea and birds in the air, for every living thing that moves on the face of Earth" (Genesis 1:26–28 MSG).

If we can get back to our original design of who God created us to be, there would not be the sexual assaults occurring like they are today. God gave us dominion over the Earth. We are created in God's image. God is love. If God is love and we are like Him, then why do we hurt one another? It is because, just like the original sin, disobedience to God and doing what God instructed us not to do causes us to feel shame and rejection. And that is the perfect breeding ground for satan to lead us into doing what we want and taking what we want.

I know these are hard things to talk about; I would rather not talk about them at all. But, due to the pain that shame and rejection has caused me and that continues to hurt such a large percentage of mankind, I cannot be silent about these things. The sexual abuse that occurs is often perpetuated by family members or friends of the family. It happens at the hands of people we trust—and people we trust around our children.

Statistics and facts show that sexual abuse usually comes from someone the victim knows, not a stranger. The "stranger danger" myth misleads the public and instills fear about the wrong source of a high risk of sexual violence. Ninety-three percent of child victims (ages 0–17) of sexual assault *knew their attacker* prior to the assault (Snyder 2000,10). So how do we stop this madness? Why does it occur? For decades, centuries and even millenna, the spirit of sexual perversion has been running rampant and destroying everything it can.

How can this abuse be changed? Education, prevention, treatment, healing, restorative justice and learning one's identity are some of the ways. Let's focus on restorative justice for a moment, since I truly believe it is one of the most underused tools we have on our toolbelt as a society. The ultimate goal of restorative justice has three parts. They include the following (Zehr 2015, 32–33):

1. Allow those most impacted by the offense to be part of the decision-making for the consequence.
2. Use healing and transformation as part of the goal of providing justice in the situation.
3. Reduce the risk of future offenses.

With this approach the victim would be heard and have the opportunity to be part of the restoration of the situation. It would allow for healing to take place for that individual. The person who committed the offense would have the opportunity to take accountability, atone for what he or she did, and move forward with an opportunity at a different life. Finally, the community would have the opportunity to heal and thrive as a safer unit of one accord.

15
The Great Cleansing

So where do we go from here? What do we do after the damage is already done? What do we do after we are already tainted and feel riddled with filth and shame, when we feel like there is no coming back from the dirt that smeared itself unto us?

We learn our true identity and worth—the one that was ours from before we were even born. We were born with worth, value, destiny and an inheritance. Some of us spend our entire lives on Earth and never know that fact. One of my goals is to share in my lifetime with as many people as possible who they truly are, not what the world has said or done to them, not what satan whispers in their ears, making them feel like they cannot escape the doom of the existence of their life. My friend, you are loved with an everlasting love. You are the beloved of God. You are cherished, and God knows your every detail.

Although you may have often felt unloved, rejected and insecure from the way you have been treated by others, there is *One* who is perfect. He gives us the Word of God, the Bible, that is inspired by God to equip, empower and encourage you in all things. If you do not know the Lord, then, as you read these words, I pray that you encounter Him in a real and tangible way. God is not a made-up deity for weak people. He is the Beginning and the End. He is the First and the Last. Before anything was created, there was God. The world is fallen and sometimes it is hard to see God today in a real and tangible way. But I promise you this: if you seek Him, you will find Him. If you truly come to a place where you want to know God, then you will find Him. It cannot be lip service. It is not like a genie in a bottle that you ask for a specific thing to happen in order for you to believe. Faith is believing though you cannot see.

Faith is there in the mystery of coming to the end of yourself and inviting God to take the wheel, to lead the way, to have Him show Himself in a way that will bring you to your knees in awe. This is why people who have been broken and come to know the Lord *cannot shut up about Him!* It really is this good. Once you know Him, you want everyone else to experience this freedom, this healing, this joy that passes all the understanding that this world has to offer. It is Jesus. He is greater than any drug, any sexual experience, anything, period. Nothing compares. That's how the simple gospel can take a murderer and make him a gentle soul. It's how a gang leader becomes a caretaker and a hope dealer. The gospel can take a drug-addicted prostitute and turn her into a pastor.

These scriptures are for you to take and own. Do not allow the enemy, satan, to have any more dominion over your life. I am declaring freedom from bondage to shame and rejection over you right now in Jesus's name. I declare it for the generations to come. You are doing a new thing. The enemy can no longer have you. You are free. Take off your shackles. Come out of your prison cell. Take hold of Christ and never let Him go, because He will never leave you nor forsake you. You will never be rejected by Him. He will never put shame on you. He will heal you of these things, just as He has healed me and many, many others. He is the God who sees you. He is a kind God.

> Oh yes, you shaped me first inside, then out; you formed me in my mother's womb. I thank you, High God—you're breathtaking! Body and soul, I am marvelously made! I worship in adoration—what a creation! You know me inside and out, you know every bone in my body; you know exactly how I was made, bit by bit, how I was sculpted from nothing into something. Like an open book, you watched me grow from conception to birth; all the stages of my life were spread out before you, the days of my life all prepared before I'd even lived one day (Psalm 139:13–16 MSG).

> We have become his poetry, a re-created people that will fulfill the destiny he has given each of us, for we are joined to Jesus, the Anointed One. Even before we were born, God planned in advance our destiny and the good works we would do to fulfill it! (Ephesians 2:10 TPT)

> But if we freely admit our sins when his light uncovers them, he will be faithful to forgive us every time. God is just to forgive us our sins because of Christ, and he will continue to cleanse us from all unrighteousness (1 John 1:9 TPT).

Do not get caught in this place of fighting whether or not you have sinned. *Every single person on Earth sins.* It is in mankind's nature. Do not compare your sin to the sins of others, either. I believe that is a tactic satan uses to try to keep people from acknowledging that they need a God at all. Satan knows that if he can keep you from salvation, then he can keep you to himself. You may think you do not belong to satan because you are not a satanist, but if you do not have Jesus, then by default you are following satan. Who do you think is whispering those awful things inside your head that makes you struggle? Once you ask Jesus into your life and repent (ask for forgiveness and turn away from your sin), satan can no longer have you. You belong to Christ. Satan will continue to try to bring you back to him, but when the Spirit of God is welcomed to come and live inside of you, everything changes. If you do not know the Holy Spirit and would like to, simply ask for Him to come and dwell inside of you.

> You may discipline us for our many sins, but never as much as we really deserve. Nor do you get even with us for what we've done. Higher than the highest heavens—that's how high your tender mercy extends! Greater than the grandeur of heaven above is the greatness of your loyal love, towering over all who fear you and bow down before you! Farther than from a sunrise to a sunset—that's how far you've removed our guilt from us. The same way a loving father feels towards his children—that's but a sample of your tender feelings towards us, your beloved children, who live in awe of you. You know all about us, inside and out. You are mindful that we're made from dust (Psalm 103:10–14 TPT).

> Listen to my testimony: I cried to God in my distress and he answered me. He freed me from all of my fears! Gaze upon him, join your life with his, and joy will come. Your faces will glisten with glory. You'll never wear that shame-face again (Psalm 34:4–5 TPT).

And this hope is not a disappointing fantasy, because we can now experience the endless love of God cascading into our hearts through the Holy Spirit who lives in us! (Romans 5:5 TPT)

This is why the Scriptures say: Things never discovered or heard of before, things beyond our ability to imagine— these are the many things God has in store for all his lovers (1 Corinthians 2:9 TPT).

16
Come Out of Hiding

When you have been beaten up numerous times by the world and by other people, you often deem people as unsafe in general and tend to want to be left alone. After decades of trying to get others to love me and value me only to have them use me and abuse me, I chose and sometimes even still choose to isolate myself from others. Some of this decision is wisdom, and some is fear. When you are vulnerable to people who are unsafe, they seek out how they can exploit and use your weakness for their gain.

The trouble is, you often do not know these people are unsafe at the time. When you come from a dysfunctional childhood, you unconsciously seek out others who have spirits familiar to those from your childhood. For example, if there was sexual perversion in your childhood, then you may be attracted as an adult to people who unconsciously carry this same perversion. Because this attraction is a soul and spirit thing, it is something you cannot see with your eyes and easily detect. It is often too late when you realize that the same toxicity from your childhood relationships has crept into your adult relationships. At that point, many people feel stuck. They think, *Ugh, I made this choice, and now I cannot get free.* Usually there is a breaking point when you do leave, but by then you are broken and sometimes feel that you are unrepairable. The good news is that there is no such thing. Unless you reach death, you are always repairable—even if it takes a lifetime.

When I look back over my life, I see all the times I was targeted for my weaknesses. I never saw that I was the one allowing people to use me in this way. By the time it was all said and done, I just wanted to be left alone. Even more so, I just wanted to die because being alone felt so lonely. When

I ended up in jail and not a single human being came to visit me, it added to the rejection from all those decades. I always cared for everyone, but no one ever cared for me. I cared so hard for others because I truly believed that we should treat people how we wanted to be treated. Until I met my David, I never had someone treat me that way. No—that may not be true. I remember some kind, gentle guys would like me even back in high school, but I rejected them. I didn't reject them because I thought they were unattractive or anything like that; it was because it was so foreign to me to be cared for. As a result, I rejected the care they were trying to give me. It felt unnatural for someone to be considerate of my feelings and to be kind to me. I was used to being controlled, manipulated and abused. Where do you think masochism and sadism and the like originate?

Research has shown that childhood abuse, especially sexual abuse, is connected with sadomasochistic tendencies. "The current study successfully expanded upon previous studies to reveal that adult sadomasochistic sexualities are linked to childhood physical, sexual or psychological abuse. And the specific type of abuse is associated with several levels of sadism and masochism examined in the study: heavy masochism, light masochism, heavy sadism, light sadism, and passive sadism" (Abrams, Chronos, and Milisavljevic Grdinic 2022, 24).

People struggle with value. When you are used to being abused or mistreated, then in a desperate attempt to gain some sense of control back, you may desire to actually be abused in order to be shown love and affection. I know this sounds counterintuitive, but follow my logic on this. Say that you are abused as a child, typically at the hands of the people you love, and you expected them to protect you against harm. Because of this harm done to you by someone you love, you correlate pain with love. You also expect abuse to keep happening to you since that is what trauma and PTSD tell your brain. In order to gain control over the situation and stop being a victim, you convince yourself that you like the pain. This process usually happens subconsciously. As a result, you have control, love and abuse all lumped together. Also, the endorphins and other chemicals that are released during pain are the same ones released during sexual arousal. So, without getting into scientific jargon, it can feel good to be treated badly because of the intense hormonal release in your body from these combined causes.

When I was released from jail, I wanted the world to think I was dead. I did not put together a funeral or post an obituary; rather, I just wanted everyone who ever knew me to forget I ever existed. It took me being all alone in prison to come to the deep understanding of God's love and presence. It is because of His love I was able to make it through that time. I went in feeling hopeless, dead and like trash, and I came out free. I wasn't free because the prison doors opened; I was free because God opened my eyes so that I could truly see. The old me was dead, and the new me was alive. This is the change that God calls us to. When we give Him our lives, we lay them down and die to who we were. We become new creations. People are always wanting to change their history and go back in time. We cannot do that, and to be honest, our history is what makes us who we are. If we want a clean slate, this is how we do it.

I came out of prison as a new creation, a new being. I closed all my social media accounts. I did not contact a single person from my old life. I prayed for God to protect me against even seeing people from my past, as I felt too vulnerable. God had shown me my identity in Him, though, and I knew that I didn't have to prove myself to anyone. I was forgiven by Christ. I was covered in His blood. I went into jail covered in filth; I was scarlet red. After my surrender and repentance, He made me white as snow, without a blemish.

I also knew that the world would still be judgmental. Most people wouldn't want to know what happened—just the story that was portrayed by the news. Instead, I chose to be hidden by the Most High. He did hide me for quite some time—until He had worked on my heart and my mind and built me up for the assignments He had for me. After He helped me work on my shame and my fear of rejection, He told me it was time. There had been layers upon layers of shame and rejection; I have had to unravel 32 years of those layers. In fact, I will be continuing to work on this area of my life for as long as it takes because we are not perfected until we are in heaven and seated with Christ.

A few years after my release, God told me He wanted me to be an influencer on social media. My response was, "Um, You know I want to be hidden, right?" He said it was time. I had become comfortable sharing my story one-on-one and in small groups. Social media, however, was a hard one. I did what any rational but scared person would do: I bargained with God. I didn't want to be disobedient, but I also did not feel ready. I said, "Okay, God, I'll do it, *but* I need You to give me another name." Immediately He gave me "Lisa Redeemed." *Lisa* means devoted to God. *Redeemed* means being saved from sin or a clearing of debt. It was so fitting, and I fell in love with my new name. It is the name of my website even today: Lisaredeemed.com. (Now would be a great time to pause and go to my website and subscribe. This way you can keep in touch.) My new name empowered me to be obedient to what God was calling me to do and be covered by Him.

He slowly brought my family back into the picture as His timing felt fit. There was so much healing I needed to do. There was so much trauma to overcome. I would sit in the presence of God, listening to worship music, and bring up a person or experience that caused me trauma or an area that needed healing and ask Him for help. I wouldn't move from that place until that trauma felt removed. For healing from trauma concerning my mom and dad, I remember it taking literally days without eating or drinking or moving from the presence of God. I would just bask in His glory, His presence and His power and light. He can heal you from anything. Are you contending for your healing? For the miracles you need? This is how you get there.

Then God started calling me to speak to larger audiences. I was afraid every time. Then I got invited to share my story with police officers. Wow! The first, second and even tenth time I was so nervous, but I spoke it. I told them I was nervous. That I had PTSD, and some of it was from involvement with law enforcement and the criminal justice system. I learned to take my pain and use it as a platform. I didn't do so in an angry, shame-on-you type of way. Instead, I simply shared my experience and how it affected me. I shared the stories of others who have shared their stories with me. I used my platform to help educate. Educating others helps to prevent more harm, and that is a big part of my mission.

Then God told me it was time to write a book, to finish the story I had started writing at 11 years old. I said, "But, You know I want to be hidden! I don't want to be an influencer or a speaker or an author. I don't want to be in the light. I don't want to be seen. I want to be hidden." He said, "That is why you are perfect for the job." This is the point where I really had to come to a *deep* level of healing when it came to the shame I had been carrying. How else was I going to write about my life—especially the way that I write, so open and vulnerable, accessible to all. I knew that not everyone would accept me or use my story for good. You need to be healed enough and know your identity thoroughly enough so that when the attacks come, you know who you are.

> Your lives light up the world. For how can you hide a city that stands on a hilltop? And who would light a lamp and then hide it in an obscure place? Instead, it's placed where everyone in the house can benefit from its light. So don't hide your light! Let it shine brightly before others, so that the commendable works will shine as light upon them, and then they will give their praise to your Father in heaven (Matthew 5:14–16 TPT).

From time to time, satan tries to knock me off course. Someone will reject me, shame me or try to remind me of who I used to be. It hurts. I'll never deny that. I go before the Lord when I cannot stand it anymore. I'll let the Father know I cannot take anymore, and He will give me rest. He is the rest for our weary souls. He and I have an understanding. I have three days maximum to feel sorry for myself, then I must get up no matter how I feel. If Jesus can die on the cross and be raised three days later, then I feel it is only right that I get up on the third day.

In 2020 I wrote my first book. It has been successful. Many have come to know the Lord and/or get free from past trauma through it. I don't get to take any of the credit, but I have seen God's hand on it all. It has been His leading and guiding every step of the way. My light is His to do what He pleases, as I am only alive because of Him, and I acknowledge this fact *every day* of my existence and will continue to do so forever more. I could not turn back because I have felt the reality of what Jesus did for me on the cross. That brought me to my knees, and I will forever be indebted to Him. He paid the price. He says the bill is paid, the sins are washed, the charges are dropped. However, it is only right that I never forget. Neither should you.

I applied for a pardon of my criminal charges a few years ago. Seeking a pardon is a very tedious process that takes years. I was already going through a really rough time with my dad dying when I received a letter informing me that I was denied and needed to wait a year before I could start the process over. I was so close to the end and then was denied. I thought for certain that I was getting the pardon. I was glad no one was home when I received the letter, because the cry that came out of me was heavy. I want that pardon so badly. I want the reality of my life to reflect what God has said: *Your slate has been cleared!* However, it was not my time for it. That is not because God said so, but because this life is hard. The process of feeling this pain and the shame it carries to have these charges is more than I can withstand sometimes. But in that process, God gets to show Himself faithful over and over—not because He makes everything in my life perfect, but because He lifts my head and reminds me who I am. We are not what the world says we are, but who God says we are: children of God. Forgiven. Righteous. Without blemish. His beloved.

17
Take My Hand

I need to make it crystal clear that this new life I have can belong to anyone. I am not some "elite" of God's Kingdom who gets special treatment. This new life is available to everyone. However, we have to partner with what God is doing. As a society, we have a huge issue with instant gratification. Our advancements in technology have made this issue even worse. We are willing to try any fad to get what we want, but only if it gets us there in 90 seconds or less. I joke about the time we are willing to invest, but when was the last time we tried to change something in our life—a new way of eating, doing more exercise or drinking more water? We buy fancy products that promise quick results, and then most of us slack off within a week or two. Why? It is because we want instant gratification. We must take the time necessary to invest in ourselves. Beginning new habits or breaking habits takes an average of 66 days before they become automatic. We must give some things some time if we really want them. Getting things instantly makes us spoiled and arrogant. When we put the work in, we will take care of that new change well.

Covid really added to isolation. Since the pandemic, the world has been telling us to stay away from others because they will make us sick. God created us out of love. We are to love Him and one another. Society, on the other hand, has become very self-driven: "I'm only worrying about me and mine." More people work from home than ever and have just about everything delivered right to their doorsteps. As much as this is a blessing that assists us when we cannot get out, some people have stopped going outside all together.

If this is you, I encourage you to get out and enjoy being around others. People are created to be together, to be social and help one another. I know it can be safer to be alone and withdrawn from the world, but that is not what your design is. That just feeds the self-fulfilling prophecy that no one cares and that you are all alone. Get out and serve your community. It feels wonderful to help others, even when you are suffering. When you are feeling down, depressed and alone, the focus is completely on "me, myself and I." That self-focus feeds itself and grows like a cancer. Getting out and serving others gets you out of your head and takes the focus off of your pain. You will find that you feel better mentally.

Take this moment and ask yourself, "Have I forgiven everyone who caused me harm?" Are you carrying unforgiveness that is making you sick? Do you constantly overthink what you said or what someone else said? Ask yourself the "why" of it all. What aren't you forgiving? Why are you overthinking?

Here are a few words of wisdom:

Think before you speak. Don't speak out of reaction to hurt. You cannot take back those words. Also, don't say that you "cannot help it." You surely can learn to shut your mouth before you open it.

Hurt people do hurt people. But if you become healed, know that healed people heal people. Do you want to hurt others or heal others? The choice is yours.

Forgiving the people who have hurt you is the most freeing thing you will ever do.

If you want your children to have a different life than you had growing up, you're going to have to heal, forgive, unlearn old things, learn new things and be transparent with your children. Educate them about where you come from. Be empowered to know you hold the power to do a new thing and change the generations to come. *You do not have to be like your parents!*

Here are some declarations (say these out loud over your life; face yourself in the mirror if you are really brave):

"I am not rejected; I am loved."
"I am free from all shame; my past does not define me anymore."
"The old me is dead, and the new me lives."
"It is none of my business what other people think of me."
"I am able to control my mouth and what I say."
"I am changing my life and that of the generations to come after me."
"My family will no longer struggle with _____." (Fill in the blank: addiction, mental health, pornography, adultery, abuse, sexual perversion, suicide, lying, pride.)

"I have perfect peace."

"My acceptance does not come from others telling me I am good enough; God says I am enough."

"I have a purpose and a future."

"I am not made to suffer; I am victorious and an overcomer."

I know that saying these declarations is at first going to seem weird and lame, and maybe you don't believe them. However, what you say matters, and sometimes you must declare a thing until you see it come to pass. In the mental health field, these are referred to as affirmations. Every word in these declarations was placed there just for you to grab hold of; you are given the authority to change how things are for you.

18
You Are Enough

In this world it is easy to not feel good enough—as a parent, a spouse, a child, a friend, an employee or even just as a human. I think more now than ever there is this illusion that there are these perfect humans, and we strive to be like them. We always fall short, though, and then we feel like failures. With social media, body modifications and camera filters, it is easy to feel like who we are is just not good enough and we need to be someone else. Recently I was glancing over an interview of a very famous actor. In it he stated that he could now see how most people who want to become actors are trying to be someone else. Even the people we daydream about becoming or about being with do not want to be themselves in their own lives sometimes.

We have these false ideals that being someone else is easier, not realizing that we all struggle with insecurities. Some people have told me that they aspire to be me. Even though this is a beautiful compliment, they don't see the hard work that goes into every day of living my life. From an outsider's point of view, it might look like I have arrived. I have not. Yes, I have come far from where I was; nevertheless, there is much more work to be done. I must continuously put work in to remember who I am today, not who I was before. Most people do not know this about me, but I need to be reminded so often of my worth to God that I got a tattoo that covers my entire back saying, "I AM the Daughter of a KING who is not moved by the world. For my GOD is with me and goes before me. I do not fear because I am HIS." What reminders can you use to help you remember that you are enough?

My friend, you *are* enough. I am enough. We are enough. We are all gifted with talents and abilities that are unique and special to us. There are times when you can't see your own abilities because you are too busy envying other people for their talents and comparing yourself with them. It hurts your feelings when you aren't good at something. This comparing and contrasting that people have been doing since the beginning of time plays a big part in why women tear each other down instead of building each other up. The truth is, my doing good doesn't mean you have to be doing bad, and vice versa. You help yourself and others a lot more when you lift people up instead of tearing them down. The person who is the prettiest in the room probably has deep and painful insecurities and doesn't know she is enough. The person who dolls herself all up on the outside might do so because she feels she is not enough inside. That doesn't mean you cannot get glammed up or look your best; but just knowing who you are on the inside is enough.

Since becoming confident in being enough, I hardly wear makeup or dress all fancy anymore. It's not that I can't do those things; I just no longer *need* to do those things to feel good enough. I used to always make sure my outside appearance looked good because I was lacking and in so much pain on the inside and didn't want anyone to know. I knew that if they knew, then they could take advantage of me and reject me. That caused me to be filled with shame. So the uglier I felt, the prettier I made myself look.

Today I am way more worried about doing a check-in with my true self and caring for her than I am about looking the part. So the next time you see me with my sweatpants on and no makeup, know that I am living my best life because I am working on being enough.

We are all walking this earth trying to figure out this thing called life and who we are. We have great moments and awful moments. Figuring life out is no easy task. We try a million different things, but most of them do not work out. People come into our lives, and people leave. We stay. We have to stay. We can't leave ourselves no matter how much we try. There is no escape. Nevertheless, we are worth putting the work in. I apologize that people have been awful to you. They, too, are trying to figure things out and failing. The good thing about failing, though, is that we can learn from it. People have such a fear of failing. I say we should embrace failing, for we know we're going to do it. We just need to learn and grow from it and do something else.

Don't be afraid to apologize to yourself and others. It takes true humility to apologize. Be honest with yourself and others. Don't hold everything in and then explode all over everyone around you. Let your true self be known and own it. And while you are trying to figure yourself out, give yourself grace. There is no formula.

Following are some words of advice that will help you with knowing you are enough:

- Focus on your strengths, not your weaknesses.
- Post reminders around you that you are enough. (I have a sign for that.)
- Read the scriptures and highlight all the ones that mention what God and Jesus say we are.
- Serve your community with your gifts and talents. You will feel better when you focus on helping others instead of on your lack.
- Surround yourself with positive people who lift you up, not tear you down.

My fellow believers, I don't want you to be confused about spiritual realities. For you know full well that when you were unbelievers you were often led astray in one way or another by your worship of idols, which are incapable of talking with you. Therefore, I want to impart to you an understanding of the following:

No one speaking by the Spirit of God would ever say, "Jesus is the accursed one." No one can say, "Jesus is the Lord Yahweh," unless the Holy Spirit is speaking through him. It is the same Holy Spirit who continues to distribute many different varieties of gifts. The Lord Yahweh is one, and he is the one who apportions to believers different varieties of ministries. The same God distributes different kinds of miracles that accomplish different results through each believer's gift and ministry as He energizes and activates them. Each believer is given continuous revelation by the Holy Spirit to benefit not just himself but all.

For example: the Spirit gives to one the gift of the word of wisdom. To another, the same Spirit gives the gift of the word of revelation knowledge. And to another, the same Spirit gives the gift of faith. And to another, the same Spirit gives gifts of healing. And to another, the power to work miracles. And to another, the gift of prophecy. And to another, the gift to discern what the Spirit is speaking. And to another, the gift of speaking different kinds of tongues. And to another, the gift of interpretation of tongues. Remember, it is the same Holy Spirit who distributes, activates, and operates these different gifts as He chooses for each believer.

Just as the human body is one, though it has many parts that together form one body, so too is Christ. For by one Spirit we all were immersed and mingled into one single body. And no matter our status—whether we are Jews or non-Jews, oppressed or free—we are all privileged to drink deeply of the same Holy Spirit.

In fact, the human body is not one single part but rather many mingled into one. So if the foot were to say, "Since I'm not a hand, I'm not part of the body," it's forgetting that it is still a vital part of the body. And if the ear were to say, "Since I'm not an eye, I'm not really a part of the body," it's forgetting that it is still an important part of the body.

Think of it this way. If the whole body were just an eyeball, how could it hear sounds? And if the whole body were just an ear, how could it smell different fragrances? But God has carefully designed each member and placed it in the body to function as He desires. A diversity is required, for if the body consisted of one single part, there wouldn't be a body at all! So now we see that there are many differing parts and functions, but one body.

It would be wrong for the eye to say to the hand, "I don't need you," and equally wrong if the head said to the foot, "I don't need you." In fact, the weaker our parts, the more vital and essential they are. The body parts we think are less honorable, we treat with greater respect. And the body parts that need to be covered in public, we treat with propriety and clothe. But some of our body parts don't require as much attention. Instead, God has mingled the body parts together, giving greater honor to the "lesser" members who lacked it. He has done this intentionally so that every member would look after the others with mutual concern, and so that there will be no division in the body. In that way, whatever happens to one member happens to all. If one suffers, everyone suffers. If one is honored, everyone rejoices (1 Corinthians 12:1–26 TPT).

19
Truly to Be Hidden

I would be lying if I said there is nothing in this world to be afraid of. Satan is always prowling around like a lion looking for someone to destroy; and he comes only to kill, steal and destroy (1 Peter 5:8; John 10:10). So *how* do we go about living our lives and living them filled with hope, joy and love? We must learn to be hidden in Christ, to be covered by Him.

I remember being in jail and getting ready for court many times. You can't take anything with you to the courthouse, so I would write scripture on the back of my court documents. That way I could read and reread them and focus on what God was saying and not on what I was seeing with my eyes. I was in a dungeon in the basement of the courthouse, similar to that of my night terrors as a child. However, when I would get in the Word of God, everything changed. One of the most important scriptures I memorized is Psalm 91. A lot of people know this psalm, but I don't know how many people truly *know* it. When you "know it, know it," you live differently. Let's take a look at this psalm. I'm going to share it in the version I memorized originally and then in my current favorite version.

Psalm 91
NEW INTERNATIONAL READER'S VERSION®

> Whoever rests in the shadow of the Most High God will be kept safe by the Mighty One. I will say about the Lord, "He is my place of safety. He is like a fort to me. He is my God. I trust in him."

He will certainly save you from hidden traps and from deadly sickness. He will cover you with his wings. Under the feathers of his wings you will find safety. He is faithful. He will keep you safe like a shield or a tower. You won't have to be afraid of the terrors that come during the night. You won't have to fear the arrows that come at you during the day. You won't have to be afraid of the sickness that attacks in the darkness. You won't have to fear the plague that destroys at noon. A thousand may fall dead at your side. Ten thousand may fall near your right hand. But no harm will come to you. You will see with your own eyes how God punishes sinful people.

Suppose you say, "The Lord is the one who keeps me safe." Suppose you let the Most High God be like a home to you. Then no harm will come to you. No terrible plague will come near your tent. The Lord will command his angels to take good care of you. They will lift you up in their hands. Then you won't trip over a stone. You will walk on lions and cobras. You will crush mighty lions and poisonous snakes.

The Lord says, "I will save the one who loves me. I will keep him safe, because he trusts in me. He will call out to me, and I will answer him. I will be with him in times of trouble. I will save him and honor him. I will give him a long and full life. I will save him."

And now my favorite version, The Passion Translation:

PSALM 91
"Safe and Secure"

When you abide under the shadow of Shaddai, you are hidden in the strength of God Most High. He's the hope that holds me and the stronghold to shelter me, the only God for me, and my great confidence. He will rescue you from every hidden trap of the enemy, and he will protect you from false accusation and any deadly curse. His massive arms are wrapped around you, protecting you. You can run under his covering of majesty and hide. His arms of faithfulness are a shield keeping you from harm. You will never worry about an attack of demonic forces at night nor have to fear a spirit of darkness coming against you. Don't fear a thing! Whether by night or by day, demonic danger will not trouble you, nor will the powers of evil be launched against you. Even in a time of disaster, with thousands and thousands being killed, you will remain unscathed and unharmed. You will be a spectator as the wicked perish in judgment, for they will be paid back for what they have done! When we live our lives within the shadow of God Most High, our secret hiding place, we will always be shielded from harm. How then could evil prevail against us or disease infect us? God sends angels with special orders to protect you wherever you go, defending you from all harm. If you walk into a trap, they'll be there for you and keep you from stumbling. You'll even walk unharmed among the fiercest powers of darkness, trampling every one of them beneath your feet! For here is what the Lord has spoken to me: "Because you loved me, delighted in me, and have been loyal to my name, I will greatly protect you. I will answer your cry for help every time you pray, and you will feel my presence in your time of trouble. I will deliver you and bring you honor. I will satisfy you with a full life and with all that I do for you. For you will enjoy the fullness of my salvation!"

References

Abrams, Mike, Aagatha Chronos and Marija Milisavljevic Grdinic. 2022. "Childhood Abuse and Sadomasochism: New Insights." *Sexologies* 13 3): 240–59.

The ACE Pyramid, Injury Prevention & Control: Division of Violence Prevention. 2014. Centers for Disease Control and Prevention. Web.archive.org. Last updated May 13, 2014. https://web.archive.org/web/20160116162134/http://www.cdc.gov/violenceprevention/acestudy/pyramid.html.

Bernard, Mihaela. 2018. "11 Common Symptoms Experienced by Victims of Childhood Sexual Abuse." PsychCentral. April 5, 2018. https://psychcentral.com/blog/practical-psychoanalysis/2018/04/11-common-symptoms-experienced-by-victims-of-childhood-sexual-abuse#1.

"Covid-19: Are You Concerned about Wearing a Mask?" n.d. The Survivors Trust. Accessed February 17, 2023. https://www.thesurvivorstrust.org/covid-19-are-you-concerned-about-wearing-a-mask.

"DSM-5 Dissociative Disorders." n.d. Traumadissociation.com/dissociative. Accessed March 29, 2023.

Holinger, Paul. 2012. "Self-Awareness." *Psychology Today*. November 19, 2012.

Lander, Laura, Janie Howsare and Marilyn Byrne. 2013. "The Impact of Substance Use Disorders on Families and Children: From Theory to Practice." *Social Work in Public Health* 28 (3–4): 194–205. https://www.tandfonline.com/doi/abs/10.1080/19371918.2013.759005.

Philadelphia DAO. 2020. "New Study Finds 1% Recidivism Rate Among Released Philly Juvenile Lifers." The Justice Wire. April 30, 2020. https://medium.com/philadelphia-justice/search?q=New+Study+Finds+1%25+Recidivism+Rate+Among+Released+Philly+Juvenile+Lifers+%22.

"Posttraumatic Stress Disorder (PTSD)." 2014. Traumadissociation.com. Accessed March 29, 2023. http://traumadissociation.com/ptsd.html.

Snyder, Howard. 2000. "Sexual Assault of Young Children as Reported to Law Enforcement: Victim, Incident, and Offender Characteristics." Bureau of Justice Statistics. July 2000. https://bjs.ojp.gov/library/publications/sexual-assault-young-children-reported-law-enforcement-victim-incident-and.

Vitale, Alex. 2018. "The New 'Superpredator' Myth." *The New York Times*. March 23, 2018. https://www.nytimes.com/2018/03/23/opinion/superpredator-myth.html.

Zehr, Howard. 2015. *The Little Book of Restorative Justice, Revised and Updated*. New York: Good Books.

Glossary

Dictionary definitions are taken from the American Psychological Association Dictionary of Psychology.[1]

addiction: *n.* a state of psychological or physical dependence (or both) on the use of alcohol or other drugs. The term is often used as an equivalent term for substance dependence and sometimes applied to behavioral disorders, such as sexual, Internet, and gambling addictions. A chemical substance with significant potential for producing dependence is called an addictive drug.

amnesia: *n.* partial or complete loss of memory. Either temporary or permanent, it may be due to physiological factors, such as injury or disease (organic amnesia), to substance use (drug-induced amnesia), or to psychological factors such as a traumatic experience. (See dissociative amnesia.)

anorexia: *n.* absence or loss of appetite for food or, less commonly, for other desires (e.g., sex), especially when chronic. It may be primarily a psychological disorder, as in anorexia nervosa, or it may have physiological causes, such as hypopituitarism.

attachment theory: a theory that (a) postulates an evolutionarily advantageous need, especially in primates, to form close emotional bonds with significant others: specifically, a need for the young to maintain close proximity to and form bonds with their caregivers; and (b) characterizes the different types of relationships between human infants and caregivers. These relationships have been shown to affect the individual's later emotional development and emotional stability.

body dysmorphia: an extreme disparagement of some aspect of appearance that is not supported by the objective evidence. There may be only a mild defect in the body feature or, in extreme cases, there may be no objective evidence of any malformation or oddity of appearance.

---

bulimia nervosa: an eating disorder involving recurrent episodes of binge eating (i.e., discrete periods of uncontrolled consumption of abnormally large quantities of food) followed by inappropriate compensatory behaviors (e.g., self-induced vomiting, misuse of laxatives, fasting, excessive exercise).

codependency: *n.* **1.** the state of being mutually reliant, for example, a relationship between two individuals who are emotionally dependent on one another. **2.** a dysfunctional relationship pattern in which an individual is psychologically dependent on (or controlled by) a person who has a pathological addiction (e.g., alcohol, gambling).

cutting: *n.* the act of cutting oneself, usually on the wrist or inside of the forearm. Often accompanied by a sense of heightened arousal and little sensation of pain, it occurs most frequently in the context of borderline personality disorder and major depressive episodes.

deliberate self-harm (DSH): the intentional, direct destruction of body tissue (most commonly by cutting, burning, scratching, self-hitting, self-biting, and head banging) without conscious suicidal intent but resulting in injury severe enough for tissue damage to occur. Although, by definition, DSH is distinguished from suicidal behaviors involving an intent to die, it is nonetheless potentially life-threatening. Typically associated with borderline personality disorder, it has also been found to occur at high rates among nonclinical populations of adolescents. It is seen as well in individuals with intellectual and developmental disabilities, in whom it is usually known by its older synonym, *self-injurious behavior.* Also called self-injury.

defense mechanism: in classical psychoanalytic theory, an unconscious reaction pattern employed by the ego to protect itself from the anxiety that arises from psychic conflict. Such mechanisms range from mature to immature, depending on how much they distort reality: denial is very immature because it negates reality, whereas sublimation is one of the most mature forms of defense because it allows indirect satisfaction of a true wish. In more recent psychological theories, defense mechanisms are seen as normal means of coping with everyday problems and external threats, but excessive use of any one, or the use of immature defenses (e.g., displacement or repression), is still considered pathological. Also called escape mechanism.

depersonalization: *n.* a state of mind in which the self appears unreal. Individuals feel estranged from themselves and usually from the external world, and thoughts and experiences have a distant, dreamlike character. In its persistent form, depersonalization is observed in such disorders as depression, hypochondriasis, dissociative states, temporal lobe epilepsy and early schizophrenia. It also often occurs as a result of a traumatic experience. The extreme form is called depersonalization syndrome.

dissociation: *n.* **1.** a defense mechanism in which conflicting impulses are kept apart or threatening ideas and feelings are separated from the rest of the psyche.

dissociative identity disorder (DID): a dissociative disorder characterized by the presence in one individual of two or more distinct identities or personality states that each recurrently take control of the individual's behavior. It is believed to be associated with severe physical and sexual abuse, especially during childhood.

dysfunctional family: a family in which relationships or communication are impaired, and members are unable to attain closeness and self-expression. Members of a dysfunctional family often develop symptomatic behaviors, and often one individual in the family presents as the identified patient.

identity confusion: uncertainty regarding one's identity, which often occurs during adolescence but may also occur at a later stage of life.

mood disorder: in *DSM-IV-TR*, a psychiatric condition in which the principal feature is a prolonged, pervasive emotional disturbance, such as a depressive disorder, bipolar disorder, or substance-induced mood disorder. Also included are mood disorders due to a general medical condition, in which attendant physiological disruptions are believed to produce the emotional changes, and mood disorder not otherwise specified, which does not meet the diagnostic criteria for any of the specific mood disorders. The term chronic mood disorder is applied when symptoms rarely remit. In *DSM-5*, mood disorders are divided into two categories: bipolar and related disorders, which include bipolar disorder and its subtypes (e.g., bipolar I, bipolar II, cyclothymic disorder); and depressive disorders (e.g., major depressive disorder, persistent depressive disorder or dysthymic disorder, premenstrual dysphoric disorder). Also called affective disorder.

posttraumatic stress disorder (PTSD): in *DSM-IV-TR*, a disorder that may result when an individual lives through or witnesses an event in which he or she believes that there is a threat to life or physical integrity and safety and experiences fear, terror, or helplessness. The symptoms are characterized by (a) reexperiencing the trauma in painful recollections, flashbacks, or recurrent dreams or nightmares; (b) avoidance of activities or places that recall the traumatic event, as well as diminished responsiveness (emotional anesthesia or numbing), with disinterest in significant activities and with feelings of detachment and estrangement from others; and (c) chronic physiological arousal, leading to such symptoms as an exaggerated startle response, disturbed sleep, difficulty in concentrating or remembering, and guilt about surviving the trauma when others did not (see survivor guilt). Subtypes are chronic posttraumatic stress disorder and delayed posttraumatic stress disorder. When the symptoms do not last longer than four weeks, a diagnosis of acute stress disorder is given instead. Changes in PTSD criteria from *DSM-IV-TR* to *DSM-5* include the following: exposure to the traumatic event may be secondhand if the event happens to a loved one or if there is repeated exposure to aversive details (e.g., as with first responders cleaning up after a disaster); the subjective criterion requiring that the person feel fear, terror, or helplessness has been eliminated; symptom clusters have been recategorized, with additional symptoms; and separate criteria have been developed for children age six years or younger.

psyche: *n.* in psychology, the mind in its totality, as distinguished from the physical organism.

rejection: *n.* **1.** denial of love, attention, interest, or approval.

resilience: *n.* the process and outcome of successfully adapting to difficult or challenging life experiences, especially through mental, emotional, and behavioral flexibility and adjustment to external and internal demands. A number of factors contribute to how well people adapt to adversities, predominant among them (a) the ways in which individuals view and engage with the world, (b) the availability and quality of social resources, and (c) specific coping strategies.

self-destructiveness: *n.* actions by an individual that are damaging and not in his or her best interest. The individual may not be aware of the damaging influence of the actions or may, on some level, wish for the resulting damage.

The behavior may be repetitive and resistant to treatment, sometimes leading to suicide attempts.

self-fulfilling prophecy: a belief or expectation that helps to bring about its own fulfillment, as, for example, when a person expects nervousness to impair his or her performance in a job interview or when a teacher's preconceptions about a student's ability influence the child's achievement for better or worse.

sexual perversion: any sexual practice that is regarded by a community or culture as an abnormal means of achieving orgasm or sexual arousal. Sexual perversion is an older term that is little used nowadays, largely having been replaced by sexual deviance or, in a psychiatric context, paraphilia.

shame: *n.* a highly unpleasant self-conscious emotion arising from the sense of there being something dishonorable, immodest, or indecorous in one's own conduct or circumstances. It is typically characterized by withdrawal from social intercourse—for example, by hiding or distracting the attention of another from one's shameful action—which can have a profound effect on psychological adjustment and interpersonal relationships. Shame may motivate not only avoidant behavior but also defensive, retaliative anger. Psychological research consistently reports a relationship between proneness to shame and a host of psychological symptoms, including depression, anxiety, eating disorders, subclinical sociopathy, and low self-esteem.

substance use disorder: a catchall diagnosis encompassing varying degrees of excessive use of a substance. In *DSM-5*, the diagnosis combines and replaces *DSM-IV-TR*'s *substance abuse* and *substance dependence* as distinct classifications, with subordinate categories of specific "use disorders" following the same pattern of consolidation: alcohol use disorder, for example, combines and replaces alcohol abuse and alcohol dependence. Other use disorders whose diagnostic criteria in *DSM-5* subsume the former abuse-dependence distinction include those involving caffeine; cannabis; hallucinogens (e.g., phencyclidine use disorder); inhalants; opioids; sedative, hypnotics, or anxiolytics; stimulants (e.g., amphetamine, cocaine); and tobacco.

suppression: *n.* **1.** a conscious effort to put disturbing thoughts and experiences out of mind, or to control and inhibit the expression of unacceptable impulses and feelings. It is distinct from the unconscious defense mechanism of *repression* in psychoanalytic theory.

trauma: *n.* **1.** any disturbing experience that results in significant fear, help-lessness, dissociation, confusion, or other disruptive feelings intense enough to have a long-lasting, negative effect on a person's attitudes, behavior, and other aspects of functioning. Traumatic events include those caused by human behavior (e.g., rape, war, industrial accidents) as well as by nature (e.g., earthquakes) and often challenge an individual's view of the world as a just, safe, and predictable place. **2.** any serious physical injury, such as a widespread burn or a blow to the head.